D1483881

ON THE GRACE AND HUMANITY OF JESUS

ON THE GRACE AND HUMANITY OF JESUS

JACQUES MARITAIN

Translated by Joseph W. Evans

HERDER AND HERDER

1969
HERDER AND HERDER NEW YORK
232 Madison Avenue, New York, N.Y. 10016

Original edition: *De la grâce et de l'humanité de Jésus,*
Bruges, Desclée de Brouwer, 1967.

Nihil obstat: Thomas J. Beary, Censor Librorum
Imprimatur: ✠ Robert F. Joyce, Bishop of Burlington
October 29, 1968

Contents

Foreword

I had hoped that *Le Paysan de la Garonne* would be my last book. Nevertheless here is another one, but one which has been written, as regards the essential point, before *Le Paysan*. It stems from the text which I had prepared for two research-meetings with the men in charge of the Little Brothers of Jesus, at Toulouse, in 1964, and which appeared in the review *Nova et Vetera* (1966, I and III). For the book edition I have tried to focus the text a little more, have revised and corrected it, while retaining its original tone, and have made some additions to it, at times somewhat technical. Perhaps I have thus made it a little heavy, but for a presentation of my views which I believe more exact. The reinterpretation which I am proposing in it of one of the theses of St. Thomas concerning the grace of Christ is, I am persuaded, valid in itself, even if in spite of all my efforts the expression of it remains imperfect. The subject treated is itself, in any case, of central importance.

It is also not without interest to several contemporary searchers, although in a perspective, I willingly recognize, quite different from my own. And it seems to me that this authorizes my effort to claim a small place in the hypotheses of research fashionable today. It may be, however, that a misunderstanding will be provoked by the few allusions which, very incidentally, I have been led to make two or three times, in my recent additions, to currents of thought which held no place in my concerns when I was preparing the two *seminars* in question. I am anxious to state that of that which occupies at present the scene, —the hubbub of those who claim to put everything in question of the traditional teaching, or the voices of those who (some attached to truth alone, some others to immobilism also) protest against the foolish arbitrariness thus set in motion, —absolutely nothing is at the origin of the reinterpretation which I am proposing here, and on which I had meditated many years. The idea came to Raïssa and me in happier days, when we were living in a serene indifference to the eddies (less violent then, it is true) of the Catholic intelligentia, and when I had still beside me, to aid me and spur me on, a gentle *counsel* beloved of God and certainly more enlightened than my poor head.

J. M.

FIRST APPROACH[1]

1. Views presented in a small research-meeting, February 10, 1964.

I. From the Virginal Conception to the Death on the Cross

1. Shall I hesitate to make this exposition because I will appear to be treading on the flower-beds of the theologians, I who am not a theologian, but a mere philosopher? In actual fact, that which I am going to say makes no claim to trespass on theological knowledge. It is the *private Meinungen,* the private opinions of a Christian philosopher, —come to the age when one's mind wanders a little, —who has a smattering of theology and considers *matters* which are the object of the theologian. But he does not consider them from the *point of view* of theology and in the perspective of theology; he considers them *in the perspective*[2] *of a philosopher,* of a *Christian philosopher.* I note in passing that the light of Christian philosophy is not, like that of theology, the light of Faith illuminating Reason in order to enable it to acquire some understanding of revealed mysteries, but the light of Reason comforted by Faith in order to do better its own work of intellectual investigation: that which authorizes Christian philosophy, at the summit of its possibilities, to concern itself according to its proper mode with matters which pertain to theology; it remains, then, subordinated to theology, but it is undoubtedly—on condi-

2. This perspective refers to that which, in their technical terminology, the Scholastics call the *lumen sub quo.* A same reality which the mind applies itself to know (*object quod*) can be seen under two different lights of intelligibility (*lumen sub quo*).

11

tion of being instructed by it—more open to a work of research and of invention; at this moment the *ancilla* becomes *research-worker*. The last word will belong naturally to the theologian. But it is the philosopher, —the Christian philosopher, in other words the philosopher in the *state* in which the concrete situation of human nature, fallen and redeemed, *requires that he be,* —it is the philosopher who in such a case will have presented to the theologian the hypothesis of research.

Finally let us leave all this, and let us say simply that I will consider things in the perspective of an old man who seeks to read the Gospel artlessly and as best he can.

PROGRESSIVE MOVEMENT AND PERFECT UNITY

2. I would like first of all to insist on the absolutely perfect *unity* of the *movement* of the life of Christ. I believe that it is necessary to regard this as a suprahuman privilege, as is impeccability. The life of Christ is a single and unique movement, from the alpha to the omega (and not, as is our life, a succession of movements more or less disjointed, of epochs which are each as the over-turning of the preceding epoch, and which entail a new setting out, sometimes a new absolute beginning). The life of Christ is an unheard-of trajectory of a perfect unity.

But a trajectory is not a serpent which bites its tail, so that the beginning is at the end and the end at the beginning. The move-ment-perfectly-one of which I am speaking is a movement, a progress, entailing passage by stages, periods or diverse phases, *from an initial point to a final point,* —from the womb of a little Virgin of Israel to the eternal Sovereignty, at the right hand of the Father.

END OF THE WORK AND END OF THE WORKMAN

3. I wonder whether, in that which concerns the Incarnation of the Word as willed by the Father (one speaks thus by appropriation, in actual fact it is the whole Trinity which has willed it), there would not be advantage in introducing into the discussion the distinction between *finis operis,* let us say the end of the work itself,[3] and *finis operantis,* the end which the one who works proposes to himself, —this is a classical distinction in philosophy.

What I mean is that the end of this divine work which is the Incarnation of the Word, is the Redemption, the work which Christ has mission to accomplish here on earth, and for which He came, in other words, the couple *Immolation* and *Resurrection:* on one side, the Cross, the Passion, the Agony, the Death,

3. The Incarnation of the Word is essentially redemptive, just as such or such a house is essentially made in order that human beings can live in it. One does not mean by this that human beings could not live elsewhere than in a house, or that the all-powerful God would not have been able to save the human race by using another means than the Incarnation of the Word. One means that itself, the Incarnation of the Word, has been willed by God and produced in existence only for the redemption of the human race (*ita quod, peccato non existente, incarnatio non fuisset: Sum. Theol.,* III, 1, 3). Contrary to Cajetan, I do not think that one can for a single moment (except by abstraction, or by leaving aside all that which, like the final cause, touches on the existential reality) consider the Incarnation independently from its real "motive," or from the end (*finis operis*) to which it is actually and essentially ordered, the redemption of the human race.

"It is to save the world," writes Cardinal Journet (*Nova et Vetera,* III, 1963), "that the Word descends into the midst of us, *propter nos et propter nostram salutem, descendit de coelis.*" (This is what I call *finis operis.*) "But by Himself alone Christ is more precious than the world, His humiliation will invoke on Him an exaltation above all creatures." (This is what I call *finis operantis.*)

—and, the third day, the Resurrection: two faces, so to speak, of a same medal.

And there is another end, —end of the workman, —to which the Incarnation and the Redemption lead through the will of the Father, and which is the divine sanction of the redemptive work accomplished by Christ: *Sedet ad dexteram Patris,* it is the royal triumph of Christ, the universal kingship which He exercises through His glorious humanity, and which will burst forth in full splendor when the cosmos will share the glory of the sons of God. This final end comes in excess in relation to the Redemption, *direct end (finis operis)* of the Incarnation of the Word; it is a surplus, but willed from the very first *(finis operantis)* by the will of the heavenly Father.

IN THE REDEMPTIVE WORK ACCOMPLISHED BY CHRIST, THE PASSION HAS NOT BEEN A MERE MEANS

4. Let us return for an instant to the work of the Redemption, in other words, to the couple Passion-Resurrection. In this couple itself the first term is ordered to the second, but as one end first attained leads to another end. It is important to note well that in the redemptive work the Passion and the Immolation have not been a *mere means.* They are an *end,* the *primary end* of the Incarnation, because they are the *victory over sin,* the accomplishment of justice towards the Father. So the Passion of the Son of God is as adorable as His Resurrection, while being ordered to the latter (the other face of the medal), which is the victory *over death.*

Notice, it is necessary to try here to be strictly exact, and I do not know if I am capable of it. For when one advances gropingly, as I am doing, one always runs the risk of pressing too strongly here or there, even if just a little bit, and of "crushing the point," as Pascal said; and I do not have the golden rule which Raïssa used almost instinctively.

Suffering, agony, death, are never an end *in themselves*. But *as redemptive, as instruments of love and of gift-of-self in the victory over sin, as exhausting on the absolutely Innocent all the suffering in which the sins of men fructify,* —that which is to satisfy in full the justice of God most holy, and to deliver the world from its sin by taking upon Himself the sin of the world, —they are an end, the primary end itself for which the Word became flesh and became as one of us.

The Passion of Good Friday is no doubt ordered to the glory of Easter, pledge of the glory of all the elect, and of the final trans-figuration of the world. But it is not a mere means, it is an end, an intermediary end. And of itself this victory over sin, over the offense or the evil of God of which the free nihilation of the creature is the cause, is something greater than the victory over death. If, in the couple Passion-Resurrection, Easter appears as a supreme accomplishment, it is because, inseparable from Good Friday, Easter, far from effacing the latter, presupposes it and contains it, by causing the scandal of God nailed to wood to emerge into the exaltation of God risen and of the creature saved; the joy of Easter, insofar as joy of the victory over death,[4] is a dazzling crown of pure silver on the bloody gold of Good Friday.

4. According as the Resurrection is not solely victory over death, but triumph of Christ entering, at the time of the Ascension, into His glory, and rendering us participants of His divinity, the joy of Easter is not a crown of pure silver, but a crown of celestial gold on the bloody gold of Good Friday.

THE STAGES OF THE LIFE OF THE LORD:
THE FIRST TWO STAGES

5. I would like to consider now the periods or stages to which I alluded a moment ago, in this movement perfectly one which is the life of Christ. It seems to me that one could count eight stages or periods in this life of the Lord. —Stage no. 1: the conception of Christ and His intra-uterine life. From the first instant of His conception He was God; He had a right to be adored; St. John the Baptist leaps, exults in the womb of his mother; the Virgin and St. Joseph adore Him. —Stage no. 2: the childhood. —Stage no. 3: the hidden life at Nazareth. —Stage no. 4: the public life and the teaching mission after His baptism and the fast in the desert. —Then (I employ the same number to recall that these two phases are as the two faces of a same medal), Stage no. 5: the Agony and the Cross; and Stage no. 5a: the Resurrection. —After that, Stage no. 6: the exercise by the glorious Christ of the universal kingship, fully and directly (although mysteriously always) over the Church, and inchoatively, indirectly, over the world, up to the last judgment.—And finally, Stage no. 7: After the resurrection from the dead, this same universal kingship exercised directly and with a full divine splendor over the glorious world.

It goes without saying that such reflections bear not on the Son of Mary *as God,* or according only as His Person is the eternal Word, but on the Son of Mary *secundum quod homo,* precisely insofar as He is born of the Virgin, or insofar as His eternal Person has acted and suffered in His earthly existence through the instrumentality of His human nature and of his human faculties, and continues in glory to act through His humanity.

Let us look more closely at these diverse periods or stages, in order to pose various questions regarding them. Some of these questions, the first in particular, have an essential importance. It may be that with some of the others I may seem to be smashing in open doors and to be examining myself sometimes concerning opinions which no one probably has ever professed (which does not mean that they could not be present more or less underground in the soul of peoples). Indeed, I am scarcely concerned about it; it is a question for me of clearing the terrain, before passing (in the subsequent chapters) to a more constructive and more doctrinal work of reflection on better delimited themes.

Let us speak first of the stage of childhood, and, already, of the conception.

6. First question: from the creation of His soul He has had the plenitude of grace, yes; but has this plenitude of grace increased? St. Luke (2, 52) says *yes: "proficiebat in sapientia et aetate, et gratia, apud Deum et homines."* He grew in wisdom, in age, *and in grace,* before God and before men. This is the Gospel. St. Thomas says *no,* —in itself the grace of Christ has not increased; it could increase only according to its effects and its manifestations.

Is there here an irreducible conflict? Such is not my opinion. It seems to me that in pushing further the distinction between the state of *comprehensor* and that of *viator,* and in placing in an interior world absolutely inaccessible to consciousness all that which was proper to the state of *comprehensor,* one arrives at new views which permit us to save at the same time the truths to which St. Thomas adhered and that which is in my opinion the obvious meaning of St. Luke.

Habitual grace has been given to the Child Jesus, immensely more elevated than in all men, and with this unique quality of being grace *in source;* but must one not consider that it itself existed at once under the two different states of *comprehensor* and of *viator?* And, consequently, why under the state of *viator* would it not have been able to increase according to the law of growth of *habitus?* I will discuss this further on. It is our absolutely central problem.

7. Second question: from the creation of His soul have all the graces of God passed through the humanity of Jesus as conjoined instrument of divinity? In my opinion it is necessary to answer yes, if one thinks only of the use made by God, as of an instrumental cause, of the simple *habitus* of grace in the soul of Christ; but it is necessary to answer no, if one thinks of *acts* of reason and of will, and of free decisions, proceeding from this habitus of grace, so that before his Ascension, nay more, from the womb of His Mother, Jesus would have exercised through the activity of His human intelligence and of His human free will a royal government over the whole universe of souls.

God can use anything as instrument in order to produce any effect. *A fortiori* it is very clear that He was able to use as instrument (instrument conjoined to divinity) sanctifying grace *as habitus,* —infused in the soul of Jesus from its creation, —in order to give all His graces to men. But *free decisions,* acts of reason and of will which proceed from this grace in the humanity of Jesus? Is this conceivable? Is it necessary to imagine that Jesus in the crib, —and from the womb of His Mother, —exercised the acts of intelligence and of will of the adult? Then it seems that we are in the presence of a kind of parody of humanity.

To say that He is in swaddling-clothes and that He governs all hearts, this is perfectly true of *this Person* who is in the swaddling-clothes, or of the Incarnate Word according as He acts divinely, in eternity, *through His uncreated will,* but not according as He acts in time *through His human will.* This is not true, —except poetically, in virtue of one of those transpositions which make the life of poetry, —of the Child Jesus *according as He is in the swaddling-clothes.* If it was as man and through the means of human acts that the Child Jesus governed all hearts, if the Child Jesus was the dispenser of all graces through the, so to speak, infinite science of His intelligence (human) and the empire of His free will (human), then how would He be the Child, the true Child of man—divine Person truly incarnate—whom the Gospel depicts and whom our heart adores? He would be rather a kind of *god disguised,* such as pagan thought could conceive Him. In short, we would be in the presence of a kind of fairy-story marvel which is unworthy of Christ and contrary to the *verus homo.*

8. Likewise, finally, if in a third question we examine ourselves concerning the universal kingship and the universal judgeship of Christ, it is clear that not only did He exercise as God, and by His eternal divine will, but also that in virtue even of the Incarnation He has as man *possessed* from the beginning the right to the universal kingship and to the universal judgment of souls. But shall we think that the Child Jesus *exercised* this right according as He was a child and through the instrumentality of human acts? To imagine that from His childhood Jesus exercised this right and directed the world and history and judged souls through the instrumentality of His human acts, while apparently He comported himself as a child, this would be to add myths to the Gospel as the authors of the apocryphal Gospels have done. The

19

right of which I am speaking at this moment, —it is after the accomplishment of His redemptive work, and finally as *sedens ad dexteram Patris,* that He exercises it as man, —in His glorious life.

THE THIRD AND FOURTH STAGES

9. Let us consider now the third stage, that of the hidden life at Nazareth. Well, must one not think that the essential of this life was *the preparation,* in itself, the preparation for His work? We have there long years of purely contemplative life—unimaginably sublime—and of manual work. And if what I have indicated a moment ago is exact, the plenitude of grace increased during that time in Christ *as viator,* and will increase in Him until the Cross. I think that at Nazareth He did not exercise only the function of universal Sanctifier in this sense that the graces of God passed to *all* through the instrumentality of the *habitus* of His infused grace, but also that from that moment He began to exercise this function through the means of His human acts. I mean that once Jesus had emerged from infancy, it is through His prayer and the intentions of His heart that the graces of God passed to some, to such or such ones whom He saw, whom He met in the occasions of life, in short, whom He knew through His "acquired experimental science."

Is it necessary to go further, and to say that external activities such as the spoken word, for example, were also the means through which He communicated the graces of Heaven? I do not think so, except in that which concerns two privileged persons: for already then, —it is that which I propose to you, it is a conjecture which I believe well-founded, —He exercised through the ministry of His word His function of Illuminator and of

Sanctifier with respect to, —but only with respect to, —Mary and Joseph; this is a point to which I would like to return another time. As regards His companions of work, if He had any, and as regards His friends, His neighbors, He prayed for them as for the other men, —and what a grace to be simply glanced at by Him! And through His love He rendered testimony to them of the love of his Father. But He did not teach them. The teaching mission, the proclamation of the Good News had not yet begun, nor the signs and the miracles which confirmed them, nor the parables through which they reached the crowds. It is to Mary and Joseph that the Gospel was announced (and in what a full manner!), —and that God and His mystery were "told." They themselves had no need of parables, or of signs and miracles. The Truth who had willed to share their life, and to be subject to them as to His father (in the eyes of men) and to His Mother (in the eyes of God and in the eyes of men), —the Truth unveiled to them all truth.

10. The fourth stage to be considered is that of the public life and of the teaching mission, —then we are in the presence of the *decisive beginning* and of the *foundation* of the redemptive work; Jesus exercises then, for a certain number of His contemporaries in Israel, who could see Him and hear Him and touch Him, He exercises no longer only through His prayer and the desires of His heart, but also through His example, through His words, through external actions and signs (and through miraculous "Signs"), His function of man through which, by reason of the acts which emanate from His plenitude of grace, the divine graces are born in souls. And this during His earthly life itself. This is what happened with regard to the apostles, the disciples, the holy women, and all those to whom He said: "Thy sins are

forgiven thee," and all the little people who thronged to hear Him. (And we can think also of all those whom in the course of the centuries the *eloquence* [5] of His example and of His words, as of His sufferings here on earth, will persuade to follow Him.) Likewise, He commences from that moment to exercise publicly His right to be by His acts of man the Illuminator of souls (let us think of all His preaching, —He has come in order to render testimony to the truth and in order to reveal it), and also (under a humble and limited form) His right of King having charge of the jurisdictional power and of the government of men, —He exercises this right insofar as He *founds the Church* and insofar as He gives it its *essential structure*. And He told Pilate, let us not forget, that He was King.

THE FOUR LAST STAGES

11. I arrive now at stages no. 5 and no. 5a, at the Passion and at the Resurrection. Here we are in the presence of *the consummation* of the redemptive work, to which the Incarnation is directly ordered. We are in the presence of the victory over *sin* and of the victory over *death*. Christ exercises fully (at the moment of His Passion and of the sacrifice of the Cross, where He is Priest and Victim at one and the same time), He exercises fully in time, for the redemption of the whole world and in the whole course of the centuries, His *eternal priesthood* before exercising it in eternity.

His Resurrection, in which He triumphs over death, and inaugurates in Himself the glorious transfiguration to which the

5. Cf. *Journal de Raïssa*, pp. 45, 49, 289-290.

whole of creation aspires, brings to an end His state of *viator*. Risen, He is no longer *viator*, He is in eternal glory. Nevertheless He will live still forty days amongst us, and during these forty days He will not exercise yet, but He will be already *in state* of exercising fully, in a manner which embraces *the whole universality* of souls, His right of universal *Sanctifier* through the humanity of whom and the free *human will* of whom, as conjoined instrument, pass all the graces that God gives.

So long as He was *viator,* He was not in a state of exercising this right *fully.* From the creation of His soul He had the Beatific Vision to an incomparably higher degree than all other men. As St. Thomas teaches, at the same time as *viator* He was *perfectus comprehensor,* which is very true but expressed in an unfortunate vocabulary, for this *comprehensor* [6] saw but did not *comprehend* the divine essence (this is impossible to any creature); and the word *perfectus* is an ambiguous word. Jesus had from the creation of His soul a Vision of God that was all that which there is of the most perfect; but to this perfect Vision there was lacking a complementary perfection which is connatural to it, —the state of beatitude or of glory, —the state which Christ, the Word Incarnate, renounced from the instant that He became incarnate and was *viator,* as He renounced many privileges of His divinity itself (this is part of the humiliation of which St. Paul speaks to the Philippians). I shall return to it further on: the Beatific Vision was as the Heaven of the soul of Christ, but a Heaven which in some manner was closed (I mean that except through the general influence and a participated light which descended from it, it did not invade the regions below the supraconscious of

6. The twofold signification, the one strict and proper, the other more broad, of the word *"comprehensor"* is indicated by St. Thomas, *Sum. Theol.,* I, 12, 7.

the spirit). It did not beatify the soul of Christ and all its powers. It was not the immediate rule and the determining principle of all the action of Christ and of all the operations of His soul. It is through the instrumentality of the faculties of human nature *in the state of way,* —faculties supernaturally "completed" or "perfected" by sanctifying grace and charity and infused science, —that passed, insofar as He acted *secundum quod homo,* and as subject to time on earth, all the activity of the Word Incarnate. All that which He expressed to others and expressed to Himself in His consciousness of *viator* required *species expressae,* concepts, notions, which referred either to His experimental science, or to His infused science, but could not come from the Vision.

On the contrary, after the Resurrection, where He ceases to be *viator* [7] and passes into the state of glory, the Beatific Vision which He has always had, and in which are seen all men of all times, takes possession of all His beatified human faculties, and becomes the immediate rule of all His action. Then He is in state of acting as free and sovereign dispenser of grace over the *universality* of souls which He sees in the Vision of God and through the infused science ruled by it, and which He can see only there, —it is only in the Vision of God, and through such an infinite infused science, that His created intellect can see at one and the same time all souls of all times, so as to exercise His lordship over the universe.

Finally, after the Resurrection He is also in state of exercising insofar as man the *universal judiciary Power,* which, as *viator,* come in order to save, not in order to judge, there was no question for Him of exercising. It's the same for the *universal kingship,*

---

7. From Good Friday onward His separated soul had ceased to be *in via.* On the descent of Christ into Hell, cf. Charles Journet, "Le temps de l'Église entre l'Annonciation et l'Ascension," *Nova et Vetera,* III, 1963.

to which, as man, He had a right from the moment of His conception, but which, come in humility, and in order to suffer and
redeem, He was not in state of exercising so long as He was
viator.[8]

12. The powers of which I have just spoken, and which,
secundum quod homo, He was in state of exercising since His
Resurrection, —power of universal Sanctifier, and of universal
Judge, and of universal King,—it is only when He will have
left the earth and will have entered the other world, the world of
God, that these diverse powers will pass to act, in the course of
the glorious stages which, in my enumeration, I have designated
as stages no. 6 and no. 7. Then the humanity of Jesus, in recompense and in sanction of the redemptive work which it has
accomplished on earth, is assumed into the trinitarian life itself,
associated, through the Word to which it is hypostatically united,
with the eternal relations of the latter with the Father and the
Holy Spirit, called to participate in the privileges of the Trinity
in the sovereign government of creatures. *Sedet ad dexteram
Patris.*

This exercise of the universal kingship or lordship, —one can
consider it first (stage no. 6) according as the humanity of the
glorious Christ puts it into act during our earthly history, up to
the universal judgment and the end of the world. Ever opposed
but constantly victorious, because it makes evil serve a greater
good, is it not fitting to say that such an exercise produces then,

8. The universal kingship was due to Him, He had a right to it from
His conception onward, by virtue of the hypostatic union, but He did
not use it during His earthly life, and the exercise of it has been the
sanction of the merit through which the work of the Redemption acquired for Him this same right. (Cf. Pope Pius XI, encyclical of 11th of
December, 1925, on the feast of Christ the King.)

although not without losses, something mysteriously *holy,* and in which uncreated Love can delight, on the side of the Church or of the Kingdom of God in pilgrimage here on earth, according as the latter in its proper life is without stain or rust while being made of sinful members; but that on the side of the world it is not thus, because the world has its own Prince who contends for it ceaselessly with Christ, and because progress in evil and progress in good are always at work there simultaneously?

With regard to the judiciary power of the glorious Christ, the latter exercises it all along the centuries through the particular judgment of which each soul is the object in the instant that it separates itself from its body; and He will exercise it at the end of the centuries through the universal judgment.

Two questions here, parenthetically. In the first place: how can love *judge?* Answer: love does not judge; it offers itself, and grace with it, to each human creature at the moment of death. And if it refuses it then, it is itself which already has called down judgment on it, for in rejecting love it makes it yield the place to *truth.*

In the second place: why the universal judgment, since each one has been previously the object of the particular judgment? Answer: it is not for the individual souls that the last judgment takes place. It is for the world, and for the entire drama of temporal history, recapitulated in a flash, with all the secret connections and the intermingled responsibilities which have been in play, and with the merits and the crimes of communities as of individuals. "Woe to thee, Corozain! woe to thee, Bethsaida! . . . it will be more tolerable for Tyre and Sidon on the day of judgment than for you. And thou, Capharnaum, . . . it will be more tolerable for the land of Sodom on the day of judgment than for

26

thee." [9] It is before that day that love will have offered to each one a last possibility for eternal life. The day of judgment is the day *of Truth*.

13. After the resurrection of the body, and with the new earth and the new Heaven, it is the last stage (no. 7) of the life of the Lord which takes place. On the side of the glorious Christ himself, this last stage is in no way distinguishable from the preceding stage, since both are in the instant-without-end of eternity, where there are no stages or periods. But it is distinguishable from the preceding phase on the side of the term attained, on the side of creatures. The time of our world has come to an end; the elect have entered into glory. The duration of matter transfigured, passed into the condition of spirit, is a discontinuous time like that of the angels. Then there is absolute and absolutely total plenitude of exercise of the kingship of the glorious Christ over the world (and over the Church, which henceforth are but one). And there there is no longer to be exercised the universal judgeship, the last judgment has already taken place.

A PROCESS OF TENDENCY

14. One knows that, in that which concerns, for example, the question of the science of Adam, a certain tendency (of Platonic origin) appeared in certain Doctors, to put in the First Man, in the Father of the whole human race, *all the perfection* already in act which will be found in the species in the course of its development.

9. Matt. 11, 21-24.

It seems to me that in that which concerns an altogether different question (the one which occupies us now, and where it is a question of the diverse periods of the life of the Saviour), an analogous tendency will be able to be found in the Christian conscience, and this time it will no longer be a matter of doctrine, as with regard to the science of Adam; it will be rather a matter of spontaneous, and insufficiently criticized, psychological disposition, which inclines us affectively towards a certain view, which will have to be later rectified.

The tendency to which I allude, and which, from a point of view a little different, I have already attacked in a preceding section, is a tendency to fold back so to speak, when one thinks of the life of the Lord, the omega on the alpha, to take back to the initial period things proper to the last stages, —such, for example, as the universal lordship not only as possessed in right by the humanity of Christ, but as exercised by it. And in the imagination of people (I speak of people poorly informed, not of the theologians) the supposed exercise of this universal lordship of the humanity of Christ from the moment that He came into the world will continue of course all His life, and will manifest itself in plenitude at the very instant of the Agony and of the immolation on the Cross. He sweats blood, He is covered with wounds, exhausted, He cries: "Why have you abandoned me?" —and this is the moment when not only is He victor over sin, which is absolutely true, but it is the moment when He triumphs in majesty, when He is *victor over death* (which is not true, since He is going to die, the victory over death is the Resurrection), and it is the moment when He *reigns sovereignly over the world.* . . . That which interests me here, is not a *doctrinal* process of tendency, which would have no sense, it is a psychological process of tendency, which refers to certain periods of the history of the collective

Christian consciousness, but can refer also to certain false steps in the history of the spiritual life of individual souls, whether it is a question of a poorly informed piety or only of some momentary excess due to affective predominances.

Take another example, one which we have already considered. One can ask oneself whether sometimes, in adoring the Child Jesus whom we hold (rightly) for the Sovereign directing the world and history, we do not think at the same time that He was such according to His very humanity and insofar precisely as born one day in Bethlehem, in a word, that He governed the universe with His infused science and His little-child's hands. *Puer senem regebat,*[10] nothing is more true, for in saying, with regard to Christ: "this child," it is the Person of the latter which one designates, the Person of the Word Incarnate, and it is indeed He who through His eternal divine will directed the old man Simeon.[11] But if one fancies that it is the Child Jesus *as child,* or through the instrumentality of His human nature and of His human faculties, who directed the old man, then we would find ourselves, as I have remarked above, before a kind of myth, and at the same time before a conception of the coming of the Saviour akin to the manner of seeing of the princes of the priests of Israel, who thought that the Messiah comes *in order to reign* (not in order to suffer). A poorly instructed Christian conscience will regard the Child Jesus according even as Child as King of the world with respect to the exercise as well as with respect to the possession of the right to reign, from the very instant of the crea-

10. At the Gradual of the Mass of the Purification: *Senex puerum portabat, puer autem senem regebat.* ("The old man carried the Child; but the Child governed the old man.")

11. Cf. *Sum. Theol.,* III, 16, 9: it is not true to say that " 'This man'— namely, Christ—'began to be' " (although—*ibid.,* 16, 10—it is true to say: " 'Christ, as man, is a creature' or 'began to be' ").

tion of His soul. One forms for oneself then an idea of Christ which differs from that of the Messiah of the princes of the priests only in this, that the exercise of His full royalty as man remains still hidden to our eyes, and in that this Son of God come *in order to reign* must pass through suffering. (Does not one take a bitter remedy in order to be cured, or does not a man pass through initiatory tests before being admitted into such or such a religious community? As if the Cross was only a bad moment that had to be passed! As if Jesus was not "in agony until the end of the world," and as if, in testimony of the *infinite intrinsic value* of the moment of time in which He suffered, He did not keep His wounds for eternity!) Thus the poorly formed and poorly instructed Christian psychology of which I am speaking made real but *invisible,* not yet manifested, this exercise of the universal lordship by the Child Jesus not only insofar as God and through His divine will, but insofar as Child and through His human will. Invisible why? Because the Lord had to pass by way of the Cross, but the Cross was only a *mere means.* To such a degree mere means (of which the good is only the good of the end) that it is on the Cross itself that the full exercise of this universal royalty first manifests itself.

THE CRUCIFIED PANTOCRATOR

15. Here we have, I fear, that which signified for many the image, so noble in itself, of the Pantocrator on the Cross (I speak of those crucifixes where it is Christ-Pantocrator who is represented on the Cross). Here I note immediately that it is necessary to avoid two extremes, one extreme which one could call *dolorism* and which consists in *separating* the moment of the Passion and of the suffer-

ing on the Cross from the *perfect unity of movement* on which I have insisted, and from the Resurrection; it seems to me that this is the case with certain Spanish Christs, one sees only the torture and one insists solely on the rending of human nature, as if God set upon that man, his Son, in order that His mission have its summit and its full accomplishment in suffering, all the rest being only accessory.

The other extreme is what one can call, in a word fashionable today, *triumphalism*. And it is that which corresponds, I believe, or corresponded, —I say in the sentiment, the instinct, the psychological reactions (and often also the practical reactions) of many—to the image of the Pantocrator on the Cross. In the instant that He agonizes and dies on the Cross and that He takes on Him the malediction of sin, not only is He victor over sin, but He reigns in majesty, He exercises fully his rights of King of glory and of Ruler of the world, He recapitulates triumphally all the grandeurs of humanity.

Rightly understood, that is to say understood as signifying at the same time as the Passion of the Lord, at once His sovereignty as God and, *by anticipation,* the glory and the plenitude of royalty of which insofar as man He will enter into possession at the Resurrection and at the Ascension, the crucifix bearing the Pantocrator is an admirable symbolic abridgment; but I greatly fear that in the common psychology (perhaps I slander it, I am not a historian), in the common psychology of the Byzantines (and of many of the Occidentals before St. Francis of Assisi) the *by anticipation* has been often forgotten. And in this case, the crucifix bearing the Pantocrator becomes the symbol of a common consciousness in which the sense of the Cross is still very insufficiently developed. The Cross on which the Christ is nailed is then the throne on which the one who insofar precisely as man exercised

31

supposedly His royalty since His conception, finds Himself elevated in order to take possession of His glory. In this psychology, in this *mentality,* the Cross becomes a mere means, indeed more, a mere episode, an accident of the glory.

I see there one of the roots of the aversion which I have often noticed in my Russian Orthodox friends towards the idea of compassion with Christ and of co-redemption through love and the Cross. What presumption, they seemed to think, what pride! No one can cooperate with Jesus, the episode of Simon of Cyrene is but a miscellaneous fact without any prefigurative import. It is not necessary only to say—in this sense that Jesus *has received no aid* from others in order to suffer and in order to accomplish the work of which He alone was capable,[12] —that He has been alone in treading the wine-press; it is necessary to say also, —in this sense that He *has in nowise given* to others to enter into communion with Him in His sufferings and in His work, —that He has been alone in carrying His Cross. Alone, —that is to say as separated from men, as apart from His Mystical Body, —alone Christ carried the redemptive Cross, means of our salvation, and stool of His glory, whereas each one carries his cross, a cross purely human, in *imitating* more or less Christ, each one for his poor small human part, but separately from His work, without *participating* through the Mystical Body in the redemptive work of Jesus. Aberrant view! What is true, on the contrary, is that each one indeed carries his own cross, but that this cross of each one is, *in reality,* a tiny little portion of the Cross of Jesus. There is but one Cross, that of the Saviour, —that Cross, *Spes unica,* which is

12. The angel of whom St. Luke speaks doubtless brought to the Garden of Olives a comfort and a consolation (like flowers or perfumes which one would throw on the body of an exhausted wrestler), but he diminished in absolutely no way His unequaled sorrow and effort.

the primary end of the Incarnation, and in which we are called to participate.

In other words, it is essential to the Mystical Body of Christ to be co-redemptive. When Cardinal Journet says that the Mystical Body is in a peregrinal and crucified state, this means that it is co-redeemer. The Incarnate Word has willed that men save the world with Him, not indeed by adding anything to His merits and to His Blood, but by *applying* through their suffering and their love His merits, His infinite merits and His redemptive Blood all along the course of time. Let me quote here a page from the *Journal de Raïssa*: [13] "I am experiencing, in a certain manner," she wrote, "that great mystery stated by St. Paul, to accomplish *that which is lacking* to the Passion of Christ.

"Being the Passion of God, it is forever gathered into the eternal. That which is lacking to it, is the *development in time.*

"Jesus has suffered only during a certain time. He cannot Himself develop His Passion and His Death in time. Those who consent to let themselves be penetrated by Him up to a perfect assimilation accomplish all along the course of time that which is lacking to His Passion. Those who consent to become *the flesh of His flesh*. Terrible marriage, in which love is not only strong like death, but begins by being a death, and a thousand deaths. . ."

And Raïssa added: "There is also an *accomplishment* of the Passion which can be given only by fallible creatures, and this is the struggle against the Fall, against the attraction of *this world* as such, against the attraction of so many sins which resemble human happiness. This gift, Jesus could not make it to the Father; only we can make it. There is a manner of redeeming the world and of suffering which is accessible only to sinners. In renouncing the goods of this world which in certain cases more numerous

13. P. 228 (25th of November, 1934).

33

than one thinks sin would have procured for us, —in giving to God our human and temporal beatitude, we give Him proportionally as much as He gives us, because we give Him *our all,* the mite of the poor woman of the Gospel."

THE LITURGY OF GOOD FRIDAY

16. Of the preceding reflections I would like to retain especially this one: the Cross is so repugnant to our nature, it is so difficult for men to admit the Cross, it is such a reversal of values, that there has been required a very long time, and that there will be required as long a time as the world will endure, in order for the Christian conscience to enter more—and finally to enter fully— into the depth of this mystery.

And likewise, our whole life is not too much for each of us in order to arrive at the end to *regard truly* the Cross of Jesus. Even if our theological faith is without defect and if we do not fall into any doctrinal error, we refuse for a long time to open our eyes on the horror and the dereliction signified by the Cross. We try to find excuses.

17. I have just spoken of a state of mind for which the Cross finds itself more or less masked by glory. It happens also, —and this time it is a more profound truth still which obscures our eyes, —that the Cross finds itself covered over and veiled for us by the tenderness of love.

Then we speak of the *gentle Cross.* The gentleness of the Cross, —there is here a very astonishing communication of idioms. *Ego,* says Jesus, *ego sum mitis corde,* —it is the gentleness of His heart which passes to the instrument of His torment. It is the tenderness of His love for us, and it is the tenderness also of our love for Him, which does not want the wood on which He has been suspended for us to be so cruel. This wood becomes flexible and compassionate, its rigor is softened by the tears of love. In this respect I know nothing more moving, and more significant, than the stanzas and the antiphon of the *Pange lingua* which the Church sings after the Reproaches of Good Friday.

Faithful cross, O tree all beauteous!
Tree all peerless and divine.
Not a grove on earth can show us
such a flower and leaf as thine.
Sweet the nails, and sweet the wood,
laden with so sweet a load!

. . . And as a lamb, upon the altar
of the cross, [Christ] for us is slain.

Lo, with gall his thirst he quenches!
See the thorns upon his brow!
Nails his tender flesh are rending!
See, his side is opened now!
Whence, to cleanse the whole creation,
streams of blood and water flow.

Lofty tree, bend down thy branches,
to embrace thy sacred load;
Oh, relax the native tension
of that all too rigid wood.
Gently, gently bear the members
of thy dying King and God.

Tree, which solely wast found worthy
the world's great victim to sustain . . .

"Dulce lignum, dulces clavos,
*   dulce pondus sustinet."*

35

Wood of love, is it not true, nails of love, bearing Love. The Lamb is dead through love, and our love responds to Him. And through the virtue of love everything becomes gentle in this Death, and even the nails, the torment, and even the Cross.

And in veiling thus to our eyes the native rigor of the Cross, it is without doubt a very great truth that love announces to us prophetically, —I mean the ineffable sweetness of the effects and of the fruits of the torments of the Crucified, and that sweetness also, that sweet-bitter sweetness of the future fruits of our own sufferings, —which sometimes (not always) will begin even to make themselves known to us on the edge of this earth.

THE HOLY CROSS

18. But in its naked reality the cross itself is not gentle, no! nor the nails, nor the lance, nor the sweating of blood, nor the *Father, why have you abandoned me*.

The cross is hard, abominably hard. By reason of our weakness this hardness can remain more or less long, more or less hidden. A day comes when it is necessary indeed that it appear, and then our mind is as if struck with bewilderment. All our bones have been broken, our being plundered, everything becomes obliterated of that which we had thought to understand. An implacable hand has passed, which has thrown us living into the abyss of death. There it is, the gentle cross.

It is nothing to say that it puts us in face of the intolerable. It is necessary to go further, to recognize that the cross, when it shows itself all naked, such as it is, it is the *inadmissible* that it imposes on us.

Is it admissible that thousands of beings made to the image of

God should perish miserably in gas chambers and sealed boxcars, crushed like vermin by other human beings? Is it admissible that there should be men who die of hunger, children who are delivered over to prostitution, immortal souls, —and such or such a one of which you have been able to glimpse the beauty, —which run in crowds towards Hell? Is it that Rachel can admit that her sons should be taken from her by death? And so many mothers, in the district of Bethlehem, whose new-born children Herod massacred?

We are too futile however to know *that which is* the suffering of others. But now, when it is we ourselves who are hit, then the scales fall from our eyes. We see suddenly that the inadmissible fills the world, and that death, be it the death of a single man, —because the immanent principle of his life is an immortal spirit, —and that tears, be it the tears of a single innocent, —because he is innocent, —are in reality things which thought refuses to admit. They are not only intolerable to the sensibility. They are inadmissible to the mind.

Happy are we if, when we are truly struck ourselves, we do not feel ourselves on the point of saying to God: since your love for me treats me in this manner, well, my love for you will render the same to you; and nothing is more easy, for you are the most vulnerable of beings.

And then a truth dawns on us: if the cross imposes on us thus the inadmissible, it is because first of all the liberty of man has imposed on God that which is *inadmissible to God:* sin, the evil of God; and God, not in order to avenge Himself, but in order to have mercy on men, and to redeem me myself, has sent His Son amongst us in order to make Him suffer in all plenitude—a certain day where all the times are gathered together—that which is *inadmissible to man,* —the inadmissible which ever since the

Fall it comes one day to each man to run smack into at the detour of the road. And that which Christ has suffered on Good Friday is a ray, one of the innumerable rays of that which hits now our flesh, and is imposed on, or, in order to speak more truly, proposed to our heart.

Indeed is there anything more thoroughly inadmissible than these scandalous realities which are at the heart of our existence here on earth and of which the name is: God made flesh, God in agony, God condemned, God spit upon and scourged, God crowned with thorns, God nailed to the Cross, God dead, God buried and risen?

Then, is it that we shall accept the unacceptable, is it that we shall admit the inadmissible? That cannot be. We shall not admit, we *shall adore* the inadmissible; one does not "accept" the cross, one takes it up, one *adores* the cross.

> *We shall adore the cross*
> *because it is the holy Cross,*
> *because we receive it from an adorable Hand,*
> *because it opens heaven to us,*
> *and because through it we suffer with Jesus,*
> *and redeem with Him our brothers.*

THE RECAPITULATION OF SORROWS

19. That co-redemption to which I have already alluded a while back, is the highest light to guide us in our night. It implies a certain recapitulation of which it is necessary now to speak, —this will be my last point.

We know that Christ recapitulates all things in Him. This signifies, in an eschatological sense, the final and triumphant recapitulation of all that which there is of grandeur and of power, of intelligence, of love, and of beauty in created being united with uncreated Being, from the moment that Christ risen sits at the right hand of the Father and delivers to Him the Kingdom. This is that glorious recapitulation on which the Russian Orthodox like to insist, and which is accomplished in the Word Incarnate before coming to its term in the transfiguration of the cosmos. Let us add that by way of regression one can find again such a recapitulation, under forms not yet glorious and in its first principle, by going back to the original point of departure, to the conception of Christ, where, from the fact of His ontological structure, He unites in Him humanity and divinity.

Now, what I would like to note, is that before the final and triumphant recapitulation there is in Christ, —this time in the suffering Christ, —*another recapitulation,* that recapitulation of "all the just blood that has been shed on the earth, from the blood of Abel the just unto the blood of Zacharias" of which it is spoken in St. Luke (11, 50) and St. Matthew (23, 35), the recapitulation, as St. Irenaeus says,[14] *of all the blood of the just and of the prophets that has been shed since the beginning,* which is also the recapitulation *of all things* wounded by sin, and recapitulated in Him, in Jesus, *in order to save them,* "in order to save, at the end, in Himself, that which had perished in the beginning in Adam."

That recapitulation has taken place, as St. Jerome remarks, "in the Cross of the Lord and in His Passion," in those last hours which begin with the Agony and end with the Death of Christ.

What does all this imply, if not that at the moment of His Passion Jesus has *recapitulated in Him all the sufferings of humanity?* He has not only borne the sins of the world, He has also borne, recapitulated in Him *all human sorrow.* "As He has

14. Cf. Charles Journet, "L'entrée du Christ dans son Église pérégri-nante," *Nova et Vetera,* January-March 1964, p. 67.

taken my will, He has taken my sadness": let us understand this remark of St. Ambrose [15] in its most profound sense.

In speaking of this recapitulation of sorrows, I am speaking of the sufferings that Jesus has *borne* as He has *borne* the sins of the world,[16] —*mystically* and through compassion, in the body and in the soul of all those (it is the entire humanity) who are His members, —I am not speaking of the sufferings which He has *personally* suffered in His own body and His own soul,[17] and which have only been the maximum point of this limitless mass of sorrows. Pascal, although this is true only in a virtual-eminent sense,[18] was right in writing, in *Mystère de Jésus:* "I was thinking of you in my agony," let us understand: not only in order to heal you of your sins, but in order to suffer with you your sorrows.

20. Let us refrain, therefore, from imagining that Jesus having taken on Him all the sins of the world, God would have set on Him as if He was alone in the world, sending on this Man a heap

15. *De Fide, ad Gratianum Imperatorem,* II, c. 7, a. 53. Cf. *Journal de Raïssa,* p. 143.

16. ". . . becoming a curse for us" (Gal. 3, 13). —*Eum qui non noverat peccatum, pro nobis peccatum fecit* (2 Cor. 5, 21).

17. It is only of these sufferings that it is a question in the *Summa Theologica* (III, 46, 5 and 6).

18. I say *virtualiter:* for the sufferings as well as the sins of each one are indeed there, but *in confuso,* in the universal Suffering and the universal Sin which Jesus has assumed in His agony in the garden (I do not speak yet of His last moment of life on the Cross. Cf. further on, pp. 142–143). And I say *eminenter:* for the Word *secundum quod Deus* sees eternally, in His divine science, the sufferings as well as the sins of each human being distinctly known in the bosom of the numberless multitude of men. And, in His agony in the garden, it is for each one, such as He knew that God sees him distinctly, that Jesus-*viator,* without Himself seeing thus, in His conscious human faculties, each individual distinctly in the bosom of the numberless multitude of men, has accepted to bear and to take upon Him the Suffering of all, as also the Sin of all.

40

of sufferings invented for Him *separately* from the common human suffering, and destined for Him *separately* from the whole mass of humanity, —so that the other men would bear for their part their own sufferings *separately* from the sufferings of Christ. Then the question would pose itself, it seems to me: why have not the sufferings of the Lamb of God delivered the world from suffering,[19] from a suffering which serves nothing since everything has been expiated by the suffering of Jesus alone, taken apart from other men?

It is indeed true that everything has been expiated by the sufferings of Jesus alone, but as Head of humanity, in communion with all other men, and recapitulating in Him all the sorrows of all other men. As I said a while back, there is but one single Cross, that of Jesus, in which all are called to participate. Jesus has taken on Him all the *sufferings* at the same time as all the *sins,* all the

19. The sufferings of the Lamb have not delivered the world from suffering, they have however modified, if I may say, the regime of suffering here on earth. On one hand, indeed, since the coming of Christianity, certain sufferings which the ancient world had certainly known, but not to the same degree, —sufferings of those persecuted for the sake of justice, of those hated, calumniated or put to death because of the Saviour (*now come*), sufferings, also, of the *disciples* whom He causes to enter in a particularly profound manner into the co-redemptive work, and let us not forget either, alas, the sufferings inflicted (on non-Christians or on other Christians) by Christians with hearts that are narrow, hard, or eager for conquest, —all this has increased the volume of human suffering. On the other hand, —without speaking of the increases of the joy of the spirit, in particular of that joy which the angels announced at Bethlehem, —and without speaking either of the moments of respite brought to human sufferings, there where they have been able, by the works of mercy, —one would say that after millennia of immobilism or of very slow progress, one sees take place on the earth, in the regions at least that God was preparing to receive Christianity, and in those where it spread, an astonishing acceleration of the activities of civilization, having for effect to liberate men from crushing conditions of life and from crushing sufferings (while new sufferings and new servitudes arise). The balance-sheet is the concern of the angels.

sufferings of the past, of the present, and of the future, gathered together, concentrated in Him as in a convergent mirror, in the instant that by His sacrifice He became, —in a manner *fully consummated* and through the sovereign exercise of His liberty and of His love of man achieving in supreme obedience and supreme union the work which was entrusted to Him, —the Head of humanity in the victory over sin.

And thus, on one hand, He has not dispensed the human race from the mass of sufferings engendered by sin (the sin of Adam and our personal sins), but He has rendered all these sufferings meritorious of eternal life, holy and redemptive *in themselves,* and co-redemptive *in the Church,* which is both His Spouse and His Mystical Body.

On the other hand, we are no longer alone in bearing our sufferings (we had never been, but we have known this only when He came). He has borne our sufferings before us, and He has put into them, together with grace and charity, a saving virtue and the germ of transfiguration. Thus human suffering is not abolished, because men, through the Blood of Christ and the sufferings of Christ and the merits of Christ, *in which they participate,* are together with Him the co-authors of their salvation. And just as they participate in the Blood of Christ and in the sufferings of Christ and in the merits of Christ according to very diverse manners, —from the manner of the Good Thief, who does but confess himself a sinner and asks mercy, up to the manner of the Virgin, and of the holy women and of St. John at the foot of the Cross, who offer themselves as victims (even and especially she who is immaculate) together with Him whom they love, —so also it is according to ways very diverse that men are the co-authors of their salvation, receiving always and giving more or less, sometimes a single final movement of consent to grace and of suppliant

42

love (and when they give more it is that they have received more). Such is the idea of the co-redemption, which designates an absolutely essential reality of the Mystical Body. Redeemed and co-redemptive, all are both, —the sinners and the saints, the great flock of the poor stragglers and the small flock of the disciples.

*   *   *

I have spoken much of the Cross, and, I fear, as a babbler and a blockhead. The poets know how to say everything in a few words. I turn to Raïssa:

> *O Cross which divides the heart*
> *O Cross which divides the world*
> *O divine Cross bitter wood*
> *Bloody price of the Beatitudes*
> *Royal Cross imperious Sign*
> *Tenebrous Cross gibbet of God*
>   *Star of Mysteries*
>   *Key of certitude*

SECOND APPROACH [1]

1. Views presented in a small research-meeting, March 25, 1964. (Text completed and developed.)

II. The Heaven of the Soul and the "Here-Below" of the Soul in the God-Man

A HYPOTHESIS OF RESEARCH

I have proposed up to this point very general views. Now I would like to attempt a second approach, in taking up again my considerations in order to try to complete them in a more systematic manner.

As a matter of fact, this involves a very difficult doctrinal recasting, of which I fear, as I indicated previously, that my abilities have permitted me to propose but a very insufficient sketch: then why this foolish enterprise, in which I feel myself entirely vulnerable?

Because I love the Little Brothers of Jesus, and because I would like very much to tell them certain things which I believe truly important on the plane of research, and which others than I could perhaps develop more fully.

And then let me tell you in confidence that the enterprise is not so foolish as it seems. If it is ventured, it is not foolish, for it is at my age that one can or that one *could* make the best effort of Thomist research, because one has half forgotten the letter and one has kept the *habitus,* which play a great deal more freely. On the other hand, being given the central importance of the humanity of Christ in contemplation and the contemplative life, a new synthesis concerning this humanity, —a Thomist synthesis in its principles and its spirit, but freed of accidental obstacles

47

due to the mentality of an epoch, and recognizing that *movement of growth,* not only as to the body but as to the things of the soul and of the spirit, is essential to every *true man,* —such a new synthesis seems entirely necessary.

What I would like especially to submit to you is a *tableau* of things which seem to me most important when we are thinking of the humanity of Jesus, of the grace of Jesus, and of the stages of His life. The reasons, the arguments which justify this tableau are perhaps contestable, —I hope indeed they are not; but it is to take a view of the tableau in its ensemble which seems to me to have the most interest in order to aid research. I add that at my age one struggles with words, and it happens that one employs an approximation in place of the exact word, which escapes one. If there are thus some defects in my vocabulary, I think that you will rectify them without difficulty. Finally, let us not forget that it is a question here of a *hypothesis of research* proposed by a philosopher working as *research worker* in the service of theology, and that it belongs naturally to theology to say the last word.

1. *The Supraconscious Divinized by the Beatific Vision in the Soul of Christ*

AN INDISPENSABLE PHILOSOPHIC INSTRUMENT

1. The question which commands everything is that of the grace of Christ. In my opinion, the customary teaching of Thomists on this point requires to be pushed further, because there is a *philosophical instrument* which was lacking at the time of St. Thomas, and which is, I believe, indispensable: a psychological notion which, as we shall see, applies in the case of Christ in a *transcendent and absolutely unique* sense, but which it was neces-

sary indeed to have disengaged first of all on the plane of the purely human and experimental analogate within our reach, I mean the explicit and explicitly elaborated notion of the *unconscious* in man; —it is our modern psychologists who have made explicit this notion, but in identifying it in general, and this is a great pity, with the *infraconscious* only, whereas there is also, and more important, certainly, although without direct interest for our psychiatrists today, a *supraconscious of the spirit.*[2] The ancients did not deny at all this supraconscious (the agent intellect, for example, exists and functions without our being conscious of it, it forms part of that which I call the natural preconscious or supraconscious of the spirit, and it is through this supraconscious that come to us the "inspirations" of which Aristotle spoke, —all this on the plane of the analogate directly accessible to our mind and proper to the *purus homo viator,* at an infinite distance from that which is proper to Christ as comprehensor), but at the time of St. Thomas the theologians had not explicitly brought out,

2. Cf. *Creative Intuition in Art and Poetry,* New York, 1953, Ch. III, Sections 6-8, pp. 90-98; Ch. IV, Sections 1-3, pp. 106-111.

Let us not forget that in the "supraconscious," —as moreover in the "infraconscious," —(which are, strictly speaking, only logical categories negatively established: that which *is not* conscious, either as above, or as below consciousness) there are many dwelling-places, in other words spheres typically different indeed, and which have sometimes between them only a purely analogical community.

Let us note further that if in *Creative Intuition* I employ preferably the expression "preconscious of the spirit," it is because, unlike the divinized supraconsciousness of Christ, the natural supraconsciousness of the spirit does not constitute a transcendent *consciousness of self* (escaping, by very reason of its superiority, from the consciousness of self, in the ordinary sense of this word, which is characteristic of the *homo viator*). Cf. further on, pp. 55-58.

Finally, as I indicate on p. 80, the spiritual preconscious or supraconscious is not only in us the natural sphere of "the spirit in its living springs," it is also the secret sphere where in virtue of the supernatural gift of God is found the seat of grace, the beginning of eternal life.

elucidated, this notion in their philosophical equipment. St. Thomas was content to say, in speaking of Christ, the "higher part" of the soul; that which I propose to say (and here is this time the transcendent analogate of our purely human supraconscious) is that it is the sphere or the world of the *supraconsciousness of the spirit divinized in Christ by the Beatific Vision.*

And this change entails very vast consequences. Once we are in possession of this philosophical instrument, this explicit and systematic notion of the divinized supraconsciousness of the spirit, it seems to me, not, indeed, that the difficulties cease, but that they become more approachable, that the image which we have of the humanity of Christ becomes more really human, and that place is made in this image (at a level below that of the divinized supraconscious) for the movement, the development, the progress, without which man is not truly man. Christ was not *purus homo;* but he was *verus homo.*

ST. LUKE AND ST. THOMAS

2. It is because he lacked the philosophical instrument of which I have just spoken that St. Thomas was led as if by necessity to treat the text of St. Luke with that which it is difficult not to regard as a certain casualness.

St. Luke says that Christ *grew in wisdom, in age, and in grace before God and before men.*

St. Thomas comments (*Sum. Theol.,* III, q. 7, a. 12): *in itself the grace of Christ could not increase;*[3] it is necessary to say

---

3. Because He was *Unigenitus a Patre, plenus gratiae et veritatis* (Jn. 1, 14). Here is then, apparently, St. John (or rather a certain consequence that one draws from his text) contrary to St. Luke. And St. Thomas chooses for St. John against St. Luke. But in reality, as we shall see, there is no opposition between their assertions.

purely and simply that Christ *did not grow* in grace or in wisdom, that He has had from the very first the maximum possible—a kind of infinity—of grace and of wisdom. (Just the contrary of what St. Luke says.) That which increased were only the effects, the *works* which manifested better and better His grace and His wisdom (ad 3).

This is the point which causes difficulty for me, and which I contest: this manner in which St. Thomas treats St. Luke. With St. Augustine and the Fathers of the Church, one can proceed thus: they have but a human authority.[4] But with the Gospel text it is altogether different, because one has to deal there with revelation itself; and very clearly St. Luke is not thinking of the effects and of the works produced; he is thinking of the *grace* and of the *wisdom* themselves, it is all the more clear as he says in the same breath: in wisdom, *in age,* and in grace. The growth in wisdom and in grace is for him in the same case as the growth *in age.*

3. Well, it is precisely this which makes necessary a general recasting. For St. Thomas the grace of Christ is at the highest degree possible from the creation of His soul. It remains absolutely immutable and without being able to grow as intrinsic quality of the soul; and it is the same for charity; and it is the same for wisdom. One has thus an *absolutely horizontal* straight line from the instant at which the soul of Jesus was created to His Death and beyond. As you will see, I do not at all reject this idea of St.

4. Cf. Charles Journet, *Le Message révélé,* Paris, 1964, pp. 157-158.
Let us not forget that as dear and venerable as are to us the Fathers and the Doctors, and the greatest among them, a million St. Augustines and a million St. Thomases will never make a St. Paul or a St. Luke. If on a given point St. Luke and St. Thomas are truly and really in conflict, the authority of St. Thomas, however high it may be, is nothing before that of St. Luke.

Thomas. But I believe that it is valid only for a certain part of the soul and of the psychic dynamism of Christ. St. Thomas thought that he had to exclude all growth properly so called of grace, of charity, and of wisdom in Jesus during His earthly life. And the matter seems to me grave, because, once again, growth is characteristic of the *verus homo* in the state of way.

Along with this it is fitting to remark that what I am going to try to say goes in the very direction in which St. Thomas was advancing, and does but extend his movement of thought; for his theology tended to bring more and more completely to light, at the same time as the divinity of Jesus, the full reality of His humanity. I believe that it has marked a decisive progress in the process which, in deplatonizing theology, marks more profoundly its *evangelical* character. In any case, he was so preoccupied with the humanity of Christ in its essential exigencies that after having first admitted in Jesus infused science only, he taught the necessity of recognizing also in Him an experimental or acquired science.[5] And it is with St. Thomas, it seems to me, that this fundamental twofold principle in Christology has decidedly imposed iself: 1) every act attributed to the Person of Christ, Second Person of the Trinity, as acting in eternity and according as He is divine, does not proceed from the Word *insofar precisely as incarnate,* it is an act of the Person of Christ which does not pass through the human nature and the human faculties of the latter, and which is common to the three Persons of the Trinity; 2) every act attributed to the Person of Christ, Second Person of the Trinity, as acting in time and according as He has taken flesh, proceeds from the Word Incarnate *insofar precisely as incarnate,*

5. "Although I have written otherwise in another place [III *Sent.,* dist. 14 and 18], it must be said that in Christ there was acquired science." *Sum. Theol.,* III, 9, 4.

and passes through the human nature and the human faculties of Christ. One can say that Jesus has created the heavens and the earth, because to designate Jesus is to designate His Person which is the divine Word [6] (and in this sense Jesus has eternally pre-existed His own existence in time). But it is not through the instrumentality of His human faculties and operations that He has created the heavens and the earth, as it is not through the intrumentality of His human faculties and operations that the Child Jesus governed the old man Simeon.[7]

If St. Thomas has not done justice to the text of St. Luke, it is, I believe, for reasons of an accidental order. In the first place

---

Nevertheless, while affirming that Christ had this experimental or acquired science, St. Thomas thought (III, 9, 4, ad 1, and especially 12, 3) that it would have been contrary to His dignity of *caput Ecclesiae, quinimmo omnium hominum,* to learn anything at all through the teaching of men. (Cf. further on, p. 117, note 73.) This thesis is inadmissible in my opinion, —it suffices to think of that which Jesus received from the Virgin and from St. Joseph in His childhood. Is it not under the direction of Joseph that He learned the trade of carpenter? And was it contrary to the dignity of the Child Jesus that Mary teach Him his first prayers, as does for her children any pious mother? As a matter of fact, in wishing to safeguard the dignity of the Word Incarnate it is His humility, His gentle humility that one disregards. How He must have been pleased to be taught by Mary, be it sometimes on things that He knew already, and better than she.

6. Likewise, and for the same reason, one cannot say "Christ is a creature" (III, 16, 8), or "Christ began to be" (III, 16, 9), although one can and ought to say "Christ, as man (*secundum quod homo*), is a creature, and began to be" (III, 16, 10).

7. With the *puer senem regebat,* of which I have already spoken in my first approach, one can bring together the two very beautiful lines of the Hymn of Lauds for Christmas:

Et lacte modico pastus est
Per quem nec ales esurit.

("He does not suffer even a bird to hunger,
and yet He was fed with a little milk.")

(and without speaking of the absence of the philosophical notion of supraconscious which I mentioned above), he had behind him (it is for the historians to trace the origins of it) a certain past of *human* tradition (I am not speaking of the sacred tradition of the Church itself, which concerns the revealed datum! I am speaking of the efforts of reason about the revealed datum). And although purely human and swarming with multifarious, contrasting, and controversial eddies, this tradition appeared as *common* among the Doctors and "experts in these matters," and at the same time as *ancient, humanly venerable,* and therefore as offering to theology positions *more probable* (it is this kind of consideration which explains the attitude of St. Thomas in the question of the Immaculate Conception). In the next place, there was (and this was rather a matter of mentality at a given epoch), the idea, tinged with Platonism, that in order to be truly man it sufficed to satisfy the non-temporal *'type* of humanity, —the notion of development or of growth in time being left in the background (whereas it is essential, and one knew it well nevertheless, or one ought to have known it, for the notion of *ratio* implies that of movement and of progress).

However the case may be, I am conscious of being faithful to the spirit and to the principles of St. Thomas in the reflections that I am proposing to you, even when they contradict his letter, and I am convinced that they do but go further in the direction in which he himself was going.

THE SPHERE OF CONSCIOUSNESS
AND THE SPHERE OF THE DIVINIZED SUPRACONSCIOUS

4. Let us return to St. Luke and to that growth of the grace of Christ which he affirms to us. It is here that it is necessary to cause

to intervene the fundamental psychological structure to which I alluded a while back. It is necessary to distinguish in the soul of Christ, during His earthly life, on one hand a world or a sphere of the *supraconscious of the spirit divinized by the Beatific Vision,* and on the other hand a world or a sphere of consciousness, or of the play of the conscious faculties functioning freely and deliberately.

Let there be no misunderstanding: when I speak of a *world of consciousness,* I am speaking of a world of which consciousness and the conscious faculties are the seat and, as it were, the sun, —but in this world there is, on one hand, *below* consciousness, the vast psycho-somatic unconscious of tendencies and of instincts, of sensations not yet elaborated in perceptions, of latent memories, etc., and, on the other hand, *above* consciousness, a preconscious or supraconscious of the spirit, in which are found the agent intellect and the sources of the intuitive activities of the spirit. It is all this that I am calling, in order to simplify, *the world of consciousness.* And this world of consciousness thus defined is the world of each one of us.

But when I speak of the *world of the Beatific Vision* or of the *divinized supraconscious* in the soul of Christ, I am speaking of a world *absolutely proper* to the soul of Christ alone, —world transcendent, —seat from which the Holy Spirit spreads His plenitude over the entire being of Christ, —domain infinitely superior to the "supraconscious of the spirit" which forms naturally a part of that which I am calling the world of consciousness.[8]

8. Is there need to add—but this is too evident—that if this divinized supraconsciousness of Christ escaped His consciousness of *viator,* it is because it was, not obscure like the infraconscious, but *too radiant,* and of a brilliance absolutely disproportionate to the power of every intellect-viator? (Imagine that I am in a cellar and am reading there a book by the light of a candle. To my left, beyond the circle of light of my candle, there is the darkness of the cellar, and if I place my book there

In order to avoid here all misunderstanding, it is not useless to state precisely that (whereas the infraconscious is made either of elements which have been driven out of the consciousness, or of elements which—such as the latent memories for example, —are a sort of infrastructure or material for it, the two of them being "unconscious" *in the sense of not integrated* with the consciousness), —on the contrary the *divinized supraconscious* of the soul of Christ, the world of the Beatific Vision was for Him a *consciousness of self* absolutely superior, let us say a supraconsciousness of self; for nothing escaped this absolutely perfect knowledge that was His Beatific Vision, it did not only show to Jesus the holy Trinity and His own divinity, it could not but show to Him also, —although not by reflection on His acts, —that His own Person, the divine Word, was the Self from which all the acts produced by His human faculties proceeded and into which led, in order to be sustained in being, all that which the external world caused them to feel or to suffer. In short, in His Beatific Vision He saw the divine Word which was His own person, and knew Himself, —through and in the divine essence, —in the most perfect and the most luminous manner possible. This was a "celestial" or "solar" consciousness of Himself, whereas the consciousness of self that He had in common with all those who share the condition of man-viator was a "terrestrial" or "crepuscular" consciousness, though illumined, unlike ours, by the infused science (cf. further on, Section 24).

I cannot distinguish anything in it, —this is for the infraconscious. And to my right there is a ray of the midday sun which, passing through a window and falling on the surface of some object in the cellar, makes there a zone of dazzling light. If I transfer my book there I can absolutely not read anything there either, I am dazzled by a brightness disproportionate to the strength of my eyes. —This is for the divinized supraconscious.)

In other words, it is necessary to say of the consciousness of Christ that which we say later on about His grace, namely, that it found itself, like His human nature, at the same time under two different *states:* insofar as He was *comprehensor* it was a divinized supraconsciousness; insofar as He was *viator* it was a consciousness in the ordinary sense which this word has in our common human life, a consciousness similar to our own as much as this was possible to a man whose person was not human but divine. And the *divinized supraconsciousness* of Christ, in other words His celestial or solar consciousness, was knowledge of self absolutely total or integral, it embraced absolutely all that which Christ was and all that which took place in Him, knew divinely (I mean through the divine essence playing the role of *species impressa*)[9] not only that which the Beatific Vision alone could see, but also absolutely all that which knew for its part, —humanly—His *terrestrial or crepuscular* consciousness.

The latter, however, had of necessity to exist in Him because He was not only *comprehensor,* but also *viator.* (Let us note, in passing, that He was *comprehensor* by reason only of an exigency proper to the hypostatic union, but that He was *viator* by reason of the very motive of this union, by reason of the very motive of the Incarnation.) And with regard to this "terrestrial" or "crepuscular" consciousness the world of the celestial or "solar" consciousness, the world of the divinized supraconscious was from the

9. In other words, giving itself in the manner of an ideative form impressed in the intellect, and causing itself to be seen thus (as the *species* imprinted in the retina by a thing which falls under the senses causes the eye to see the beauty of the world) without the intellect having, in this unique case, to produce starting from the intelligible matrix imprinted in it an interior word or concept, —what concept engendered by a created mind could "represent" God? (The *species inditae* of the angels are as weak in this respect as the concepts of the human intellect.)

57

point of view of man-*viator* a sort of total "unconscious," but in a sense entirely different from that in which this word is said of the infraconscious.

All this being well understood, one sees at the same stroke how, in order not to confuse language (and because our language is necessarily that of the earth), my vocabulary has been established. When, speaking of the soul of Jesus, I say *consciousness* or *world of consciousness,* I employ this word exclusively in the sense of *consciousness of Christ as viator,* "terrestrial" or "crepuscular" consciousness, consciousness of human mode. And in that which concerns the consciousness of Christ as comprehensor, instead of saying "celestial" or "solar" consciousness, I say simply *world of the divinized supraconscious* or *world of the Beatific Vision.*

Finally, if it is a question of the *world of consciousness,* which Christ had in common with us, —well, whereas in us this world is wounded by sin, on the contrary in Christ it was free not only of original sin but of all sin,[10] and immaculate, and incomparably holy from the beginning.

5. In conclusion of all the preceding considerations, let us say that the *world of the vision or of the divinized supraconscious* was that of the soul of Christ as *comprehensor:* and the *world of*

10. With the blessed it is the *Beatific Vision* which is the ground of their impeccability. *"Visio beata per se immediate et formaliter destruit omne dictamen defectuosum . . . Unde formaliter et immediate destruit omnem potentiam, et radicem peccandi."* John of Saint Thomas, *Cursus Theologicus, in I-II De Beatitudine,* quaest. 5, disp. 2, a. 5, no. 21, ed. Vivès, t. V, p. 252.

In Christ it is not the same. The reason of His impeccability was His *divine Person itself,* because it is the supposit which is the Agent just as it is the Existent. *"Et ratione talis principii Christus est impeccabilis ab intrinseco; quia ejus persona est divina, nec potest operari, et influere concursu personali et proprio in actionem quae sit offensa, et aversio ab ipsamet persona"* (*ibid.,* no. 11, p. 248).

consciousness such as I have defined it was that of the soul of Christ as *viator*.

Christ was at the same time *comprehensor* and *viator*.[11] If one does not admit in the soul of Christ a difference of level, a *heaven* of the soul, but supraconscious, for the state of *comprehensor*, and a *here-below* of the soul, the here-below of consciousness and of the conscious and deliberate operations, for the state of *viator*, I believe that one is inevitably led to wrong the one or the other of these two states.

I admit, therefore, these two worlds in the soul of Christ, corresponding to the two simultaneous states of *comprehensor* and of *viator* in which He found himself. I think that there was clearly a certain communication between these two states and these two worlds: to be sure, since it is the *same nature* and the *same faculties* which were under the *state* of comprehensor and under the *state* of viator. Hence this communication. Hence also the particular characteristics which, without changing the essential constitutive of the states in question, affected in Christ the state of *viator*, from the fact that He was also *comprehensor*, and the state of *comprehensor* from the fact that He was also *viator*.[12] But I think that there was also *a certain incommunicability* between them, which caused that the *content* of the supraconscious heaven of the soul was retained, could not pass into the world of consciousness, or of the here-below, except, as I indicated in the first approach, by mode of general influx, and of comforting, and of participated light. In short, there was, so to speak, a *partition* between the world of the Beatific Vision and that of the conscious faculties, —but translucid partition which let pass, through the light of the infused science which participated in the evidence

11. Cf. *Sum. Theol.*, III, 15, 10.
12. Cf. further on, pp. 82–86.

of the vision,[13] as through the virtue and the attractions of the sovereign peace which reigned in the heaven of the soul, a vivifying radiance over all the faculties, —proper climate of the unity, of the humble but absolute certitude of self, of the stability, of the impeccability, of the suprahuman power of the soul of Christ. Through a glazed window we do not see the sun but its light and its heat pass. (And "translucid" does not say enough. This partition opened when Jesus wished to cross it.)[14]

If I speak thus of a kind of imperfect partition between the world of the divinized supraconscious and the world of consciousness, it is, in the first place, because there is *absolutely no possibility of expressing through concepts,* neither to others nor to oneself, that which is known through the Vision; and it is in the second place because there was not in Christ, during His earthly life, that glorious transfiguration and terminal divinization of the *world of consciousness and of the entire soul* which the Beatific Vision effects in the blessed, and through which the Vision becomes the immediate rule of all their action. Christ was *comprehensor,* He was not *blessed* (since He had come in order to suffer!).[15]

13. Cf. further on, Section 20.

14. I indicate this a few lines below. Cf. also further on, Section 28.

15. In one sense, —in the sense that He had the Vision of the divine essence, —He was indeed blessed (III, 9, 2 ad 2), and even during His Passion (46, 8), in that which St. Thomas calls the higher part of the soul and which we call the divinized supraconscious of the latter. But, St. Thomas teaches, there was no *derivatio* or *redundantia,* there was no repercussion of the higher part on the lower part, this is why the Beatific Vision has not at all prevented the suffering of Christ, in His Passion, from being greater than all the sufferings (46, 6). —*Dum Christus erat viator, non fiebat redundantia gloriae a superiori parte (animae) in inferiorem, nec ab anima in corpus* (46, 8). In this assertion of St. Thomas one finds an indication, quite inchoative no doubt and merely sketched, but valuable, of the notion of "partition," in the soul of Christ, between the world of the Beatific Vision and that of the conscious faculties, which I introduce here, and to which I attach a particular importance.

6. The immense—and closed, in the sense in which I have just indicated—world of the Beatific Vision, let us say therefore that it was the Paradise of the soul of Christ, a world from which, consequently, suffering was absent, —but which was a *supraconscious* world. This Paradise *was there* because Christ was *comprehensor*. It was *closed* because Christ was *viator*. (Actually, by that part of His soul Jesus was already in Heaven, not on earth. Since He had there the *same Beatific Vision, the same degree of grace, the same degree of charity,* that He will have in Heaven for eternity).

Through His infused prayer He experienced this world; He entered with His consciousness, in order to experience it in an ineffable manner, into this world where He was alone with His Father and the Trinity. It was, so to speak, the nest in which He took refuge, but He brought there also the suffering coming from here on earth, His compassion for the sufferings of men, His anguish over their moral misery and the offenses to His Father that are their sins; and He contemplated there the redemptive work and the sacrifice for which He had come.

And at the moment of the Agony and of the Passion He can no longer enter there, He is barred from it by uncrossable barriers, this is why He feels himself abandoned. That has been the supreme exemplar of the night of the spirit of the mystics, the absolutely complete night. The whole world of the Vision and of the divinized supraconscious was there, but He no longer experienced it at all through His infused contemplation. And likewise the radiance and the influx of this world on the entire soul were more powerful than ever, but were no longer seized at all by the consciousness, nor experienced. Jesus was more than ever united with the Father, but in the terror and the sweat of blood, and in the experience of dereliction.

2. *In What Sense the Habitual Grace of Christ Was Unlimited in its Order*

THE FORMAL EFFECT PRODUCED BY SANCTIFYING GRACE IN THE SOUL OF CHRIST (AS COMPREHENSOR)

7. I would like first, as a beginning, to comment on the texts in which St. Thomas speaks to us about the grace of Christ (cf. *Sum. Theol.,* III, q. 7, a. 9, 10, 11 and 12).

He tells us there, not with regard to the hypostatic *grace of union* of which we are not speaking (it is clearly infinite, since the Person of the Word is infinite), but with regard to the *habitual grace* or sanctifying grace of the soul of Christ, the only one of which we are speaking, —St. Thomas tells us (q. 7, a. 11) that the grace of Christ is *finite* as entity, or as to its *entitative being, secundum quod est quoddam ens,* which is very evident, this I understand well; but he adds that *according to the "ratio" or the formal aspect proper to grace, secundum propriam rationem gratiae,* one can nevertheless call it infinite, because from this point of view *it is not limited.*

Of this second assertion one finds an explanation in a preceding article (a. 9), in which he tells us that Christ had necessarily to have the maximum of grace, *as fire, which is cause of the heat in all hot bodies, is at the maximum of heat.* And in this article 11 where he declares that *according to the proper "ratio" of grace* the grace of Christ can be called infinite or not limited, he tells us likewise: *just as the light of the sun can be called infinite, not doubtless according to its being, but according to the "ratio" of light, because it has all that which can belong to the "ratio" of light.*

I confess that these reasons scarcely satisfy me: perhaps because I feel myself annoyed by the examples taken from the physics of the time; perhaps because if I see well that all the graces received by men are participations in the grace of Christ, I see less well that from the earthly life of the latter it was thus because the grace of Christ would have caused them intentionally by its acts (except in that which concerns a small number of men who had the privilege of seeing Him and of hearing Him, —in all the other cases, God gave then His graces to men in using as instrument, it seems to me, only the *habitus* itself of grace present in the soul of Christ).

I would like, therefore, to try to find another manner of explaining how a thing can be *finite* as to its entitative being and *infinite* under another relation. All that I have been able to do, — and it is already quite presumptuous—is to try to construct a little philosophical scaffolding, doubtlessly very incomplete, but which will suffice, it seems to me, for my purpose in the present discussion.

8. In order to construct my little scaffolding, I make use, on the one hand, of an example for the imagination, on the other hand, of certain remarkable philosophic formulas employed by St. Thomas.

The example for the imagination is supplied to me by geometry. It is the case of a curve such as the hyperbola which approaches more and more a straight line which is its asymptote, without ever attaining it.

The formulas employed by St. Thomas I find in Part III, q. 7, a. 12. In the body of the article he tells us of the *ultimate perfec-*

tion with which a form can be possessed by a subject; and in the ad 1, he tells us that *in the forms themselves* (*much more still than in natural quantity* [in contradistinction to mathematical quantity]), in the forms themselves *it is necessary to consider a certain term beyond which they cannot pass.* (*In ipsis formis consideratur aliquis terminus, ultra quem non transgrediuntur.*)

After having meditated a little on all this, I would like to enunciate a principle in which I reconstruct things to my fashion, and which in order to be brief I shall call the *principle of the asymptote.*

Each time that a form possessed by a multiplicity of subjects grows more and more in perfection in approaching unceasingly, —but without being able ever to attain it, —this same form such as it is possessed by a certain typical (asymptotic) subject, it is necessary to say that in this subject it is found at *a point of perfection supreme and unsurpassable,* or in other words, that it is there *beyond all measure, beyond the endless series of all the possible limited degrees,* in a word, in a manner *unlimited in its order.*

Let us note parenthetically that this identification between the notion of *ultimate perfection* and that of *beyond all measure* or infinite in its order, is found explicitly in St. Thomas: that which attains to the ultimate perfection under which a certain form can be possessed (q. 7, a. 12), possesses this perfection beyond all assignable measure, the form in question is not given to it *secundum aliquam certam mensuram* (q. 7, a. 11).

I return to my principle of the asymptote, in order to illuminate it by example.

Take for example the thousands of people who have read the *Summa Theologica,* or heard the *Don Giovanni* of Mozart. They understand the work in question more or less perfectly, one can, therefore group them by the mind in a series in which the understanding of the work is more and more perfect, and this series can be prolonged without end: never at any point of the series will one attain the understanding of the *Summa* such as it was in St. Thomas, or the understanding of *Don Giovanni* such as it was in Mozart. In St. Thomas and in Mozart (who are an asymptote with respect to the series) this understanding was at a point of perfection supreme and unsurpassable, it was there in a manner unlimited in its order, beyond the endless series of all the possible limited degrees.

It is the same if you consider, for example, the endless series of counterfeit bank-notes which forgers can make more and more perfectly: never will the "form"—the extraordinarily complex characteristic ensemble of distinctive qualities and traits—possessed by any of these counterfeit notes more and more perfectly made attain this same form such as it is possessed by the *authentic bank-note,* which is, as it were, an asymptote with respect to the whole series.

Here is established the concept of which we had need. By what word to express it, by what word to qualify the form such as it exists in the asymptotic subject—St. Thomas, Mozart, the note of the Bank of France—where it is found at a supreme or unsurpassable degree, beyond all assignable measure, beyond the endless series of all the possible limited degrees?

If one considers the etymological formation, the word "transfinite" would be perhaps the one which would suit best, —although in a general fashion it is very bad to divert a word proper to a given lexicon (here, the mathematical lexicon) in order to employ it in another lexicon (the philosophical lexicon) in a sense completely different.

This does not mean that we cannot employ from time to time

this word "transfinite," but I think that the best thing is to employ quite simply the word *infinite* (in its order) or *unlimited* (in its order), the parenthesis "in its order" being able, moreover, in many cases to be understood without inconvenience, from the moment that the sense has been well established.

9. And now, in what manner and on what condition can the word in question be applied to the grace of Christ? This is what we have to examine now, it is our second problem. Before entering into detail, I would like to make a general remark with regard to the distinction of St. Thomas between the grace of Christ *taken according to its "esse" or its entitative being* (in this case it is finite, he says, and this is indeed evident) and the grace of Christ taken *secundum propriam rationem gratiae* (it is then that he says that it is infinite).

It is the manner in which St. Thomas expresses the second member of the distinction, it is the *secundum propriam rationem gratiae* that I have trouble with. Therefore, where St. Thomas says *secundum propriam rationem gratiae,* I shall say: *according to the formal effect which grace produces in the soul in which it is received* (or as to the mode according to which it renders it participant in the deity).

And in the soul of Christ (and of Christ alone) this formal effect is double. It is either related to the mode (infinite) proper to the *divine Person of Christ,* this in the supraconscious paradise of the soul of Christ; or else subject to the mode (finite) proper to the *human nature* of Christ, this in the world of the conscious here-below of the soul of Christ.

And in the first case, in the paradise of the soul of Christ, it is there, and there only, that from the earthly life of Christ grace was *transfinite* or *infinite in its order.* In the second case, in the here-below of the soul of Christ during His earthly life, His grace was finite in its order, or below the point of supreme and un-surpassable perfection. All this is going to become more clear, I hope so at least.

THE GRACE OF CHRIST AS COMPREHENSOR

10. The idea that I propose to you therefore, is that, just as the human nature of Christ was at once under two different states, the state of *comprehensor* and the state of *viator,* so also the grace which perfects this nature, the habitual grace of Christ was also under these two different states of *comprehensor* and of *viator.* This is my fundamental presupposition.

Why is it so? Because, —case absolutely unique, due to that unparalleled event which is the Incarnation of the Word, — the human nature itself of Christ was at once under these two states. It is difficult to understand and to imagine? Certainly. But it is a fact which it is necessary to recognize from the moment that one admits the fact of the Incarnation.

And since grace is a *habitus* (entitative) given *by mode of nature,* it is necessary indeed that the grace received by the human nature of Christ and which perfects this human nature, —which is at once under the state of *comprehensor* and under the state of *viator,* —be itself also under these two states, let us say better, under the state of final consummation, in which the soul possesses God through the vision, and under the state of way, in which the soul advances towards God.

How is this possible and conceivable? Whether it is a question of the human nature of Christ perfected by grace, or of the grace which perfects the human nature of Christ, this is possible and conceivable only on two presuppositions.

In the first place, on condition of recognizing in Christ a fully divinized supraconscious, a *heaven of the soul* of which the content does not descend into the sphere of the consciousness and of its reflex grasps, and in which the soul lives already the very life of eternity; and on the other hand, a sphere or a domain centered on the consciousness (it is the whole psychism of other men) and in process of divinization, a *here-below of the soul,* in which the latter lives the life of time and of earthly pilgrimage.

In the second place, on condition of recognizing that between the heaven of the soul of Christ and the here-below of His soul (the consciousness in the sense in which I am employing this word)[16] there was not an absolute discontinuity, a partition preventing all communication, but a certain discontinuity, a sort of partition, due precisely to the absolute transcendence of the divinized sphere of the soul, and allowing to pass from the heaven of the soul to the here-below of the soul only a general comforting and a participated light.

So long as these two presuppositions are not clearly recognized, one cannot conceive that the same habitus of grace finds itself at once under two different states, that of final consummation in which grace is of infinite degree, and that of way, in which it is of finite (and increasing) degree. And this is doubtless why this idea of the double state of grace in the soul of Christ, which is in no way incompatible with the Christology of St. Thomas, and does but complete it, has remained in the background[17] in St. Thomas himself.

16. See above, pp. 54–60.
17. Or, at least, barely sketched. Cf. above, p. 60, note 2.

In order to aid our imagination before a case so absolutely unique, I shall try later on to find some remote analogies, inevitably very deficient, in our ordinary psychological world. I am afraid that they are of little worth. It is doubtless better to content ourselves with a simple imagery. Let us imagine an enormous giant, so tall that his head is higher than the layer of clouds from which falls an abundant rain on the earth. He climbs a mountain, whose summit is also higher than this layer of clouds; there he will be able to stretch himself out and sleep in the azure. Soaked by the rain, his body, while waiting, strides along under the clouds, from which it will emerge completely only at the end. But from the beginning his head is already in the azure and it enjoys it fully.

11. Let us consider now the grace of Christ as *comprehensor*. According as it was under the *state* of *comprehensor*, —in the supraconscious paradise of the soul of Christ, —the grace of Christ, which remained *finite* as to its *esse* or to its entitative being, was under another relation, and insofar as proportioned to the Beatific Vision of Christ, infinite in its order and could not grow.

Let us recall that the Beatific Vision was not given to Christ as the fruit of a previously acquired merit. It was given to Him from the very first, as an exigency of the hypostatic union, and, so to speak, as a gift from the latter. From the moment that the Word becomes incarnate, it is necessary that His human nature participate in the Deity to the sovereign degree possible, in short, that it be elevated to the state of comprehensor, that is to say, that it see God.

There then is the Beatific Vision in the soul of Christ. And the habitual grace of Christ, which is given to Him from the very first, must be, according to the formal effect that it produces in the soul, proportionate to this Vision. It must be consummated grace, rendering, through the *lumen gloriae,* the intellect of Christ capable of being informed by the divine essence taking the place of *species impressa.* It must be thus *there where the Beatific Vision is received,* that is to say, at a certain level in the soul of Christ, or in a sphere absolutely proper to the soul of Christ (because while being *verus homo* He is not *purus homo*), —in that part of the soul of Christ where everything is *ruled immediately by the Vision and centered on the Vision,* in other words, in the *supraconscious paradise* of the soul of Christ.

And it does not suffice to say that there grace is *consummated.* It is necessary to say moreover that there grace is *infinite in its order,* or at an unsurpassable degree. For being given that consummated grace renders man, in an achieved and terminative manner,—as is the case for all the blessed,—God by participation, so that it frees to this extent the deified human nature from the limitations and finitude proper to its created essence, one must conclude that *there where the Person is infinite* (as in Christ), consummated grace must go further still, and cause the human nature to participate in the Deity according to a mode accorded to *the divine Person himself who sustains in being this grace,* that is to say, according to a transfinite or infinite mode. (Let us not forget indeed that *actiones sunt suppositorum,* it is the person or the supposit which acts and operates, and likewise it is the person which receives fundamentally, or as existential subject, the grace which perfects his nature, —let us say, in the case of Christ and of His uncreated Person, it is the *divine Person* who sustains in being the grace which perfects His assumed human nature.)

To have a habitual grace *infinite in its order or to the point of supreme and unsurpassable perfection* (asymptotic) is thus a privilege unique to Christ, since every other man has a *finite* person, and since accordingly in every *purus homo* grace, even the consummated grace proper to the blessed, is also of *finite* mode, at a given degree of perfection which admits always above it the possibility of a greater degree. On the contrary, in Christ as *comprehensor,* in the paradise of the soul of Christ, in the world of the divinized supraconscious, grace was, from the creation of the soul of Christ, at the asymptotic degree, beyond all assignable measure, at a degree to which can attain, no matter how great it may be, the grace of no mere creature, angel or human being; it was at the point of perfection supreme and unsurpassable, *secundum perfectissimum modum qui potest haberi* (q. 7, a. 9), *in maxima excellentia quae potest haberi* (q. 7, a. 10).[18] So that it could absolutely not increase (cf. q. 7, a. 12).

12. That which I have just said of the grace of Christ *as comprehensor,* it is necessary to say also of the *operations* and of the operative *habitus* which proceed from this grace.

We shall say, therefore, that the *Beatific Vision* of Christ as *comprehensor,* or in the supraconscious paradise of the soul of Christ, was from the beginning at the point of perfection supreme or unsurpassable, or beyond all assignable measure, it was infinite or unlimited in its order.[19]

18. Thus the text of St. John (1, 14) to which St. Thomas refers, accords fully, in reality, with that of St. Luke (2, 52) instead of requiring that the latter be sacrificed to it (cf. above, p. 50, note 3).

19. St. Thomas does not discuss explicitly this point, he says only (that which is equivalent) that the soul of Christ saw the Word more perfectly than any other creature (III, q. 10, a. 4). In Part I (q. 12, a. 7) he says that the light of glory cannot be [entitatively] infinite (this is why the blessed cannot *comprehend* the divine essence). At this moment he is not treating of the questions which concern the Incarnation. But is it not

This is not to say, clearly, that the Vision of Christ-*compre-hensor comprehends* the divine essence or knows it as much as it is intelligible. That is reserved to God alone, and to the *absolute infinity* of His intellection of Himself by Himself.

Christ-*comprehensor* does not *comprehend,* He *sees* the divine essence, but He sees it at a degree of perfection *transfinite* or *infinite in its order,* whereas all the angels and the blessed (and more perfectly than them all, Mary in Heaven) see it at a degree *finite* in its order.

And this Vision, as I have already noted, is *absolutely simple* (indivisible), and *absolutely inexpressible in any concept, any idea,* even as to any one of the particular things which it makes known. How has one been able sometimes to forget this? As if the Vision was not absolutely indivisible and could be parcelled out! It is precisely for this reason that, in the soul of Christ during His earthly life, —where, as in every *verus homo viator,* His intellect functioned through the means of ideas which He expressed to Himself and expressed to others, —absolutely nothing of that which was known by Him in the Vision could directly pass into the sphere of consciousness, be directly known by Him in such a way that He might express it to Himself and express it to others, —whether it is a question of His own divinity or of the moment when the Second Coming will take place (St. Mark, 22, 32). With a thousand-dollar bill you cannot get for yourself a cup of orange juice which an automatic dispenser furnishes you for a quarter. You will die of thirst if you do not find a money-

---

obvious that in Christ it must be with the light of glory as it is with grace itself, and that, *finite* in its *esse* or in its entitative being, it must nevertheless in such a case be called *transfinite* or infinite under another relation ("asymptotically")? As I say in the text, the soul of Christ did not *comprehend* the divine essence (God alone comprehends it). But it *saw* it infinitely better than any of the blessed sees it.

changer, someone who gives you change for your bill. That which in the case of Christ played the role of money-changer, and enabled Him to know in the sphere of His consciousness, to express to Himself and to express to others something that He knew already (under a mode incomparably superior, but supraconscious) in His Beatific Vision, was His infused science.

Let us add that the state of *comprehensor* does not include only the *Beatific Vision,* it includes also *Beatific Love;* and in Christ-*comprehensor,* this Beatific Love which proceeds from a grace infinite in its order is also infinite or unlimited in its order, —not indeed of the same infinity as uncreated Love, but according as it participates in this uncreated Love to a degree of perfection supreme and unsurpassable (asymptotic), beyond all assignable measure.

Thus therefore, *habitual grace* infinite in its order, *Beatific Vision* infinite in its order, *Beatific Love* infinite in its order (and which possesses an infinite value; I say value, I do not say merit, for there is merit only in the state of way [20]), and further, *wisdom* infinite in its order, according as the habitus of infused science and of infused wisdom was in the paradise of the soul of Christ at the supreme degree of perfection, —well, all this is included by the state of *comprehensor* under which exists the human soul of the Incarnate Word.

And from all this, all possible growth is excluded. All this, being from the beginning at the highest possible degree, can only remain immutably at this degree without ever increasing.

13. Here is the *horizontal straight line* which St. Thomas had in view and which continues without end since the creation of

20. On the infinite merit of Christ, see further on, p. 75 and Section 30 (p. 136, note 12).

the soul of Christ—not only until the last instant of the earthly life of Jesus, but *in the centuries of centuries,* for this treasure of infinite grace remains absolutely the same in Heaven as it is already on earth, and it can absolutely not increase.

These are clearly things entirely suprahuman. They stem from the fact that Christ is not *purus homo,* and they bear testimony to this fact.[21]

But they do not at all prevent Christ from being *verus homo*— *if* they are valid *only* for the part of the soul of Christ which during His earthly life was above the world of consciousness, above the world of free and deliberate action, and of abstractive and conceptualizing intelligence.

Let us put our horizontal straight line, and all the treasures of glory of which it is the symbol, *in the paradise of the soul of Christ,* in the world of the fully divinized supraconsciousness of Christ, where it remains shut up during the whole duration of the earthly life of Christ, then we understand how at the same time He is *verus homo,* and we understand that in the world of consciousness and of free and deliberate action, as of the natural supraconscious of the spirit, and of the subconscious, let us say in order to simplify, in the *here-below* of the soul of Christ—in other words, in the interior world that Christ has, as does every man,

---

21. As also to the connected fact that nothing can be conceived greater than the *Unigenitus a Patre* and the grace with which He is full (cf. above, p. 50, note 3).

To deny the existence of this "horizontal straight line," or of the state of *comprehensor* to the highest degree which, from the creation of the soul of Christ, has remained unchanged in Him for always, would be to misunderstand the hypostatic union itself. Thus we agree, but in understanding it as is fitting, to the saying of St. John Damascene: "Those who say that Christ advanced in wisdom and in grace as receiving an addition, do not venerate the Union." *De fide orth.,* I. III, c. 22 (cf. *Sum. Theol.,* III, 12, 2, obj. 3).

through human nature *in the state of way,* —we must picture to ourselves another straight line, an *oblique straight line,* which starting from below (from a "below" which is already a summit in relation to every mere creature), *rises* towards the horizontal straight line, and signifies that ascensional movement, that growth, that progress of which St. Luke speaks to us, that growth in grace and in wisdom, as in age, which is an essential property of every *verus homo.* This oblique straight line rises, all during the time of the earthly life of Christ, towards the horizontal straight line, and finally it meets it (I shall return to this in Chapter IV, Section 30) at a very precise point, exactly at the moment when Jesus utters on the Cross His sixth and His seventh words, declares that all is consummated and delivers up His soul into the hands of the Father. At this moment He is as *viator* at the same degree of grace and of charity at which He was, and will remain as *comprehensor,* —and since He is still *viator* He has an infinite *merit,* as He has an infinite love, —the work of the Redemption for which He has come is consummated. During all the previous time, it was in preparation and in process of becoming; it is consummated at that moment.

THE GRACE OF CHRIST AS VIATOR

14. Let us consider, therefore, this ascending oblique straight line of which I have just spoken, and which, in contradistinction to the *paradise* of the soul of Christ, belonged to the world of the *here-below* of the soul of Christ, which was proper, in Him as in all men on earth, to the human nature in the state of way.

My fundamental presupposition, you remember, is that just as the *human nature* of Christ found itself at once under two *states,* the state of *comprehensor* (in the paradise of the soul) and the state of *viator* (in the here-below of the soul), —so also the habitual grace likewise found itself in Christ under these two *states,* the state of *comprehensor* or of final consummation (in the paradise of the soul) and the state of *viator* or of earthly pilgrimage (in the here-below of the soul of Christ).

And as we have seen, this grace was *infinite* in its order under the state of *comprehensor* and in the paradise of the soul of Christ. But in the state of *viator* and in the here-below of the soul of Christ, it is necessary to say that it was *finite* in its order, —up until the last moment (exclusively) of the earthly life of Christ.

As I have already noted above (Section 10), we are here in the presence of a case absolutely unique, due to this unparalleled event which is the Incarnation of the Word. I have tried to indicate also why it had necessarily to be thus. This does not make the question easier. But it obliges us to recall that of the mystery of the Incarnation as of every revealed mystery we can attain only "some understanding." That which constitutes in all this discussion the major difficulty is not the fact that a nature which finds itself simultaneously under two different states behaves in a different manner under one state and under the other (nothing is more logical indeed), or that a habitus (grace is an entitative habitus) which finds itself simultaneously under two different states should have a formal effect of different degree under one state and under the other; that which constitutes the major difficulty,[22] is the fact that a nature or a habitus *finds itself simultaneously* under two different states: which is precisely the case before

22. This difficulty did not at all stop St. Thomas in that which concerns the nature of Christ; one does not see why it would stop us any more in that which concerns His grace. Cf. *Sum. Theol.,* III, 15, 10 and ad 1.

which the revealed datum places us with Christ, at once *compre-hensor* and *viator*. During His earthly life He found Himself simultaneously under these two states, which are not only differ-ent, but opposed, and which would be even totally incompatible if each of them was taken, not in its essential constitutive only, but in the plenitude of its properties and of its consequences.

That grace and the infused gifts should have been able to find themselves at once under a state of unsurpassable perfection in the heaven of the soul of Jesus, and under a state of growth in the here-below of the latter is understandable, however, if one recalls that when one says that grace, charity, wisdom, grew in the here-below of the soul of Christ-*viator,* one does not at all say that God infused into it there a grace, a wisdom, and a charity which *in themselves would have been more and more great.* How would this have been possible, since in the paradise of His soul Jesus already had grace, charity, the gift of wisdom, at their sovereign and eternal degree, under the state of limitless plenitude due to the condition of a *comprehensor* possessing an infinite Beatific Vision; and since, on the other hand, these supernatural gifts, which there could not grow, whereas they grew in the here-below of the soul, were each a single and same infused habitus? That which one says, is that these same infused habitus, which from the creation of the soul of Jesus had from the very first spread out totally in the paradise of this soul, with a limitless plenitude which excluded all progressive deepening and there-fore all growth, on the other hand *took root more and more pro-foundly in the subject, according to the law of growth of infused habitus,* —it is in this sense that they *grew,* —when they passed into the here-below of the soul, where they found themselves, as in us, under a state of finitude due to the condition of the subject-

77

viator in which they took their being and their dimensions.[23] The *esse* of infused habitus consists indeed, as St. Thomas says, in *inesse,* and depends thus on the conditions of the subject which receives them; in a subject-*comprehensor* it is an *inesse* free from the conditions of the earth (an *inesse* infinite in the case of Christ as *comprehensor*); in the subject-*viator* it is an *inesse* submitted to the conditions of the earth (hence a finite *inesse* in the case of Christ as viator.).[24]

The fact remains that such a duality of simultaneous states as different as Heaven and earth is absolutely proper to the Word Incarnate, and it is entirely impossible to find in our experience examples which give a more or less satisfying analogical idea of it. It is not useless however, I believe, to think of examples (ex-

23. This law of growth of habitus does not prevent, of course, that on the other hand God, when He wills, infuses more abundantly, at such or such a moment, grace and charity into a soul, just as He infuses them into such a soul more abundantly than into such another one, in the sense, this time, in which the gift that He makes is considered *in itself,* and not only as to the depth of its taking root in the subject. However great they may be, these supernatural gifts remain *finite* in every created soul, except that of Christ.

24. "How can the same infused indivisible habitus (grace, wisdom, charity) be at the same time at its maximum in the free paradise of the soul of Christ, and grow in the penumbra of the here-below of His soul? The answer is to be sought in the law of growth of infused habitus. It comes about through their progressive taking root in the subject: *'accidentis esse est inesse . . . nihil est aliud caritatem secundum essentiam augeri, quam eam magis inesse in subjecto,'* St. Thomas, II-II, q. 24, a. 4, ad 3. St. John of the Cross speaks of the purification, not *of* the theological virtues (this is impossible), but of the faculties of the soul *through* the theological virtues. If it is a question of Christ-viator, one will say that the progress of the infused habitus came about in Him through their more profound taking root in proportion as the increasing difficulties of His mission required of Him acts of charity more intense." Charles Journet, *Nova et Vetera* 1967, III, pp. 236-237. I am happy to owe to Cardinal Journet this final precision which illumines the whole question. (Note of the second edition.)

amples from below) which, however inevitably deficient and unsatisfying they may be, reassure us nevertheless as to the validity of the paths in which our reasoning proceeds.

Let us think then for example of a man in whom the operative habitus of an art has to act under two different states: the artist in question finds himself *under the state of creation* when starting from recollection in creative intuition he composes a work, and *under the state of didacticism* or *of reflexive explanation* when he teaches pupils the laws of his art. This being given, it may be that under the first state his habitus—the *same* habitus of art—finds itself at a degree altogether inspired and under the second state at a degree most mediocre. In this example, however, one has to deal with activities which are not simultaneous, but succeed one another.

Take now a man who has undergone in his early childhood psychic traumatisms now completely forgotten, and which have produced in his unconscious (infraconscious, "Freudian unconscious") serious troubles. There is in him, consequently, a discontinuity between the *conscious state of psychic activity* and the *unconscious state of psychic activity*. Let us suppose that this man possesses the moral virtues. They will be able to exist at a very high degree under the first state and at a very low degree under the second, whether it is a question of the perverse and regressive tendencies in which he delights in his unconscious, or of the compensations of pride and of egoism, indeed of sadism, which without his suspecting it his unconscious introduces into the exercise (conscious) itself of his virtues. Here we have two simultaneous states, but this is possible only thanks to *a sort of partition but not complete* between the world where his conscious activity and that where his unconscious activity (centered on dream and on instinct) have respectively their seat.

One can think, finally, of the example of a man like Father Surin, whose intellect found itself at once under a state of mystical union that was most lofty and under a state of psychosis bordering sometimes on madness. This same intellect had under the first state an activity of a degree altogether superior (of which we have for fruit and for witness the admirable spiritual writings of Father Surin); and under the second it was at a degree of functioning that was most low, when it abandoned itself to the obsessions whose seat was an unconscious in full pathological disorder. And there also the simultaneity was possible only thanks to a sort of partition (but not complete) in the soul.

In our two last examples, it is to the world of the *infraconscious* that it was necessary for us to have recourse. The supraconscious functions in us only in the zone of "the spirit in its living springs," where the world of conscious activity has its hidden sources. And it is there also (that which pertains to the *pneuma* rather the *psyche*) that is the seat of grace, and that in certain souls a habitual union with God establishes itself, too profound to be perceived. But it is too clear that a world of the *supraconscious divinized by the Beatific Vision* could occur only in the unique case of the Word Incarnate.

In reflecting on the diverse examples which I have just proposed, I have, let us be honest, the discouraging impression of a laborious floundering. It is better, therefore, to forget them and to think of the sole analogy that I would like to retain, —infinitely deficient, certainly, but just the same more appropriate. Let us think of a musician of genius, prodigiously gifted from infancy, —of a Mozart. Would not one say that in the soul of the child Mozart music itself was there, divine essence hidden in the heaven of that soul, and absolutely inaccessible to consciousness, whereas in advancing from year to year, and from work to work, in the knowledge and the possession of his art (in causing to grow in him his virtue of art) he drew near again through tears that inaccessible paradise of angelic infancy where it seemed that everything had been given him from the very first?

15. After this parenthesis let us return to our purpose, and to the consideration of the grace of Christ as *viator*. In the view that I was proposing a moment ago when we were considering the paradise of the soul of Christ, it is according as the habitual grace of Christ was proportioned to the Beatific Vision that it was infinite in its order, there where in the soul of Christ everything was *ruled immediately by the Vision and centered on the Vision,* —in that region of the soul of Christ, therefore, which (because while being *verus homo* He was nevertheless not *purus homo*) was absolutely proper to Him, and which was in Him the sphere of the *divinized supraconscious,* that which we have called the paradise of the soul of Christ.

But it is precisely that which could not be the case for Christ as *viator,* and according as while not being *purus homo,* He was nevertheless *verus homo.* For in every man in the state of way (if at least he does not behave in a manner unworthy of man) the functioning of human nature and of its faculties is *centered on reason* (even when the latter is moved by higher gifts). It was necessary, therefore, that according to the formal effect which it produces in the soul the grace of Christ be proportioned, no longer to the Vision, but to the functioning of human nature centered on reason, —I say there where in the soul of Christ as *viator* everything was centered on reason (elevated itself by the gifts and the inspiration of the Holy Spirit), in other words in that which we have called the world of consciousness or of the here-below of the soul of Christ.

And in that sphere, where grace has not for formal effect to produce in the soul an *achieved* or *consummated* participation in the divine nature, or to render *terminatively* man God by participation, human nature was not freed or delivered in any way of the limitations and of the finitude proper to its created essence. Human nature, therefore, imposed there, necessarily, its finite mode, —limited to all that which it received as to all that which emanated from it, to all that which could come to it from above as to all that which it could produce as radical principle of operation.

This means that in the here-below of the soul of Christ the grace which the divine Person sustained in being and through which His assumed human nature participated in the divine nature, was accorded or adapted not to the mode of the infinite divine Person but to that of the finite human nature, and was necessarily *finite* as that human nature itself, —finite not only as to its entitative being but also as to the formal effect produced by it in the soul (under the action of God as first Cause, of course, and according to the measure determined by the divine wisdom, —measure more elevated, from the creation of the soul of Christ, than in any *purus homo,* but nevertheless finite, and destined to become greater and greater in proportion as Jesus grew in age). This grace under the state of way was finite in its order, or below the point of supreme perfection.

16. Is it not a law of the hypostatic union that the Word, from the moment that He makes His own the human nature in taking in relation to it, —He, infinite Person, —the place of a human person, assumes that created nature according to all the exigencies which are essential to it? It is an essential exigency of human nature to have a created *esse,* and the human nature of Christ has

a created *esse*, in addition to the uncreated *esse* of the divine Person.[25] It is an essential exigency of human nature *in the state of way* that the grace received by it be a grace finite like it. And it was thus in Christ taken as *viator*, in the state of way, in other words, in the sphere of the here-below of the soul of Christ.

We have seen a while ago that the *non purus homo* requires that the grace of Christ *as comprehensor* be infinite in its order, or to the point of supreme excellence. We see now that the *verus homo* requires that the grace of Christ *as viator* be finite in its order, below the point of supreme and unsurpassable perfection.

For every mere man there is an essential discontinuity between the grace proper to the state of way and consummated grace or glory, proper to the state of term or of beatitude. In order to pass from the one to the other it is necessary to cross the threshold of death (and Jesus also has passed this threshold, in order to enter into glory, into the full bloom of the normal consequences of the Vision).

For Christ, who during His earthly life was at once *comprehensor* and *viator*, the discontinuity of which I have just spoken existed also, but insofar as it bore on two different *states* of a same entitative habitus (the word *difference-of-level* would be perhaps more accurate, in such a case, than the word discontinuity). And it was necessary indeed, consequently, that that which was *per se primo* constitutive of the state of *comprehensor* reside in a supra-conscious region of His soul, whereas that which was essential to the state of *viator* should be at work in the conscious region, in the sphere of the here-below of this same soul. It was necessary

25. I am referring here to the works of Father H. Diepen (especially "La critique du Baslisme selon saint Thomas d'Aquin," in the *Revue Thomiste,* 1950), and to the explicit text of St. Thomas in the opusculum *De Unione Verbi Incarnati.* Cf. *The Degrees of Knowledge* (new translation), second version of Appendix IV.

indeed that Jesus should have a *supraconsciousness of self* absolutely ineffable and absolutely incommunicable, and, below this supraconsciousness, a *consciousness of self* of the same type as that of every man-*viator* (consciousness which not only causes that each one of us perceives obscurely, but also permits him to say to himself that he is a man). This consciousness of self not only enabled Christ to perceive obscurely, it permitted Him to say to Himself (by what process, this is one of the great questions that I shall have to tackle a little later on) not only that He was man but also that He was God.

Before going any further, let us note well, in order to avoid all misunderstanding, a thing moreover evident, since Christ is at once God and man. If the state of *comprehensor* under which His humanity found itself manifested more completely the *non purus homo,* and if the state of *viator* manifested more completely the *verus homo,* it is clear nevertheless that under one state as under the other, in the two cases Christ was at once *verus homo* and *non purus homo.* This said, I continue.

From the fact that He was not only *verus homo,* but also *non purus homo* (to the point of being *comprehensor*), the difference between Him and other men manifested itself necessarily even in the sphere of the here-below of His soul. It is thus that this *viator* had a grace and a wisdom which, although finite (according even as He was *viator*) were higher than those of any other man, however holy he might be. And not only was His grace higher than that of any other man, but it had a *unique modality,* which came from the fact that the supposit or the person which sustained it in being was the divine Word; there was, therefore, *connaturality* between it and the Person whose nature it superelevated; nay more, it is from the Trinity that it proceeded, therefore also *from this same Word* which insofar as divine lived with the trinitarian

84

Life and which insofar as incarnate lived with the human life and was the Person of Christ. Let us say that the grace of Christ, at whatever degree that one considers it, and contrary to that of any other human (or angelic) being, was grace *in source*.

This *viator* had neither the theological virtue of faith nor that of hope [26] (since in the divinized supraconscious of His soul, there where He was *comprehensor*, He had the Beatific Vision, and in the world of consciousness He had an infused science which participated in the evidence of the Vision); this *viator* had infused science, He was impeccable, etc.

And from the fact that He was not only *non purus homo* but also *verus homo* (and even *verus homo viator*), the difference

26. He had, nevertheless, hope (but not as theological virtue) *respectu aliquorum quae nondum erat adeptus* (*Sum. Theol.*, III, 7, 4).

I wonder whether on the subject of faith one could not say something analogous. Christ did not have theological faith, but His *confidence* in the heavenly Father was absolute (together with the "faith" of being hearkened to by Him); and was this not a certain analogate (not theological) of faith? And is it not owing to His very experience itself, in His own soul, of such a virtue of total confidence and certitude, that so often the faith (theological) of which He taught the necessity, —the faith *in Him,* and in the Father, and in the Spirit, —appears in the Gospel under the veil, so to speak, of the confidence through which it manifests itself in the occasions of life, in other words according as it is present and engaged in its *practical application,* which is the confidence of being hearkened to? (One can think that Luther, in his doctrine of faith-confidence, let himself be taken in by these appearances.) Cf. Matt. 9, 22: "Take courage, daughter; thy faith has saved thee"; 9, 29: "Let it be done to you according to your faith"; 15, 28: "O woman, great is thy faith! Let it be done to thee as thou wilt"; 21, 21: "If you have faith and do not waver"; Mk. 4, 40: "Why are you fearful? Are you still without faith?" And again, Matt. 8, 13: "Go thy way; as thou hast believed, so be it done to thee"; Mk. 11: 24: "Therefore I say to you, all things whatever you ask for in prayer, believe that you shall receive"; Lk. 8, 50: "Do not be afraid; only have faith and she shall be saved." —The fact remains that a great number of other texts, especially in St. John, relate to *faith* taken in itself, independently of the confidence in the granting of a request (and inattributable to *the Truth itself revealing itself*).

85

between Him and other men (I mean those who are in Heaven and enjoy the Vision) manifested itself also even as regards the sphere of the paradise of His soul, which was closed in the sense that I have said, so that the Vision of God could not have for Him its normal consequence: beatitude and glory. This *comprehensor* had not a spiritual body, like that of the blessed when it will be reunited with their soul, and like His own after His Resurrection: He had like us a perishable body of flesh, He had hunger and thirst, He wept with sorrow and with compassion, He was exposed to fatigue, to suffering, to anguish, to temptation, to death. And the interior world of His consciousness was centered, not on the Beatific Vision as with the blessed, but, as with us, on reason, subjugated, not supplanted, by the gifts of Heaven.

17. The habitual grace finite in its order, according to the exigencies of the state of way, which Christ had as *viator* or in the sphere of the *here-below* of His soul, was from the creation of His soul more elevated than that of any mere creature. And it did not cease to *grow* all through His earthly life.

And that which I say of the grace in state of way, in the sphere of the here-below of the soul of Christ, it is necessary clearly to say it also of the *charity* in the state of way, in the sphere of the here-below of the soul of Christ. For the operative habitus of charity was in Christ, just as the entitative habitus of grace, under two different *states,* under the *state of final consummation* in the paradise of the soul of Christ, and under the *state of way* in the here-below of the soul of Christ. It was there, therefore, in the sphere of the here-below of the soul of Christ, a charity *finite* in its order, and whose acts remained below the point of supreme perfection, therefore a charity which did not cease to *grow* all along the course of the earthly life of Jesus: every act of charity, for Him as for other men, causing, by way of merit, an increase of the virtue of charity, so that this immense finite charity did not cease to grow, and to merit, and to grow, all along the earthly life of Christ, from His first act of charity. The merits of Christ insofar as *viator*[27] did not cease either to grow, like His charity, until the last moment, where the merit becomes infinite, as we shall see presently.

Finally, it is necessary to say that the wisdom was also in the soul of Jesus under the two *states* mentioned, and that the wisdom of Christ as *viator*, —that wisdom which included at once the infused science and the gift of Widsom, —was just as the grace and the charity of Christ *as viator,* a wisdom finite in its order, and which did not cease to grow all the time that He lived, up to the moment when He entered into His glory, and when it gave place to the wisdom of Christ as *comprehensor,* wisdom infinite in its order, or to the point of perfection supreme and unsurpassable, which, from the moment He is in glory, is no longer shut up in a supraconscious paradise of the soul. For in the soul of the glorious Christ there is no longer either sphere of a celestial supraconsciousness in which the vision was shut up, or sphere of an earthly consciousness which was not invaded by the vision. There is no longer anything but a celestial interior universe, at once conscious and illumined completely by the vision.

27. Merits not only for Himself (with regard to the increase of grace and of charity, and finally with regard to the glorification of His body and the entry into the universal lordship), but also *for other men and for their salvation,* because all the merits which accumulated progressively in Christ as *viator* have been summed up and recapitulated in the sacrifice of the Cross and its infinite merit.

III. The Infused Science of Christ

1. *Questions Concerning the Infused Science Itself*

RETURN TO THE FIRST AND SECOND STAGES
OF THE LIFE OF CHRIST

18. It is of the infused science of Christ that I would like to speak to you now. In order to enter into this great subject, —you recall that in our first approach we have distinguished eight stages in the life of the Lord, —a few words first of all concerning the two first stages.

Firstly. From the creation of His soul, Jesus has received the *Beatific Vision*.[1] There was in Him, during His intra-uterine life,

1. Since the creation of His soul Jesus knew fully, through the Beatific Vision, —but only in the supraconscious paradise of His soul —all the members of His Mystical Body, and—there also only, in the heaven of His soul, or insofar precisely as comprehensor—enveloped each one with His infinite charity. It is thus that, in the perspective which I am proposing, it is necessary to understand the following lines of the encyclical *Mystici Corporis*: "The knowledge and love of our divine Redeemer, of which we were the object from the first moment of His Incarnation, exceed all that the human intellect can hope to grasp. For hardly was He conceived in the womb of the Mother of God, when He began to enjoy the Beatific Vision, and in that Vision all the members of His Mystical Body were continually and unceasingly present to Him, and He embraced them with His redeeming love." (Pius XII, *Mystici Corporis, Acta Apostolicae Sedis,* 1943, p. 230). —From the instant of the creation of His soul it has been thus, according to my view, for the *supraconsciousness already celestial, the heaven of the soul* of Jesus, but not for His consciousness of viator, which He had in common with other men and which depended on the *human mode* according to which He lived in the *here-below of His soul.* Cf. further on, Section 31.

only that which I have called the paradise of the soul, the world of the *Vision,* which from the very beginning has been at the point of supreme and unsurpassable perfection; and this world was all the more supraconscious, all the more incommunicable to consciousness, as there was not yet any consciousness properly so called below it, but only the confused sensations, not accompanied by reflex consciousness, which the little Child conceived receives in the womb of His mother. One can, therefore, say that while He was in the womb of Mary He was also in the closed paradise of His soul, where He led a celestial life, while His body and the here-below of His soul were still in the prenatal state.

Secondly. From the creation of His soul He has received also *infused science,*[2] through *species infusae,* ideative (intuitional) forms infused (unlike concepts abstractively formed under the light of the agent intellect): *species infusae* which one must conceive as internal determinations passively received from God by the intellect, and which the latter puts in second act (act of operation) when it passes to exercise *ad imperium voluntatis.*[3] This infused science of Christ, of the same type as that of the

2. Cf. John of St. Thomas, *Curs. Theol.,* Vivès, VIII, disp. 11, a. 2 —Christ, as St. Thomas tells us, had the infused science in order that [in the paradise of His soul] His intellect would be perfect according to all its possibilities (cf. *Sum. Theol.,* III, 11, 1; 12, 1). But there is more. Far from the infused science having been rendered superfluous by the Beatific Vision, it is on the contrary because the Vision is an immediate knowledge of the divine essence, in which the latter is united to the created mind *sicut intelligibile intelligenti,* that which exceeds the proportion of this mind (*Sum. Theol.,* III, 9, 3, ad 3) that the soul of Christ, in order to know and to judge *juxta modum suum connaturalem proportionatum* (John of Saint Thomas, *loc. cit.,* n. 15), had to possess the infused science, below the Vision; and this is the case also—in a mode of existence altogether different—for the life of Christ entered forever into His glory.

3. Cf. *Sum Theol.,* III, q. 11, a. 5, ad 2. —In the body of the article, St. Thomas notes that: "the medium between a pure power and a completed act is a habitus."

separated souls [4] and of the angels, but higher and more luminous than that even of the angels,[5] was not at the state of exercise always in act; it was at the state of *habitus* (III, q. 11, a. 5) or of proximate disposition to use infused *species* in making them pass to the act of operation; and it included even a plurality of habitus,[6] in other words, it was in Christ according to "a mode *connatural to the human soul*" (same article).

St. Thomas tells us [7] that it extended not only to all that which man can know through the virtue of the light of the agent intellect, but also to all that which is transmitted to us by divine revelation, whether it is a question of the gift of wisdom and of the other gifts of the Holy Spirit, or of the gift of prophecy,[8] since also indeed, as I have already noted, it diversified itself into a plurality of habitus (a. 6).

To all this we can only subscribe, —in what sense, I am going to say in a moment. But because St. Thomas had made explicit neither the notion of supraconscious, nor that of a kind of partition, in the soul of Christ, between the sphere of the supracon-

---

4. *Ibid.,* III, 11, 1, ad 2.

5. *Ibid.,* a. 4.

6. Cf. III, 11, 6. —According to my view, it is only *in the here-below of the soul of Christ* that His infused science (in the undivided state in the paradise of His soul, where it found itself under a mode connatural to the human soul *divinized by the Vision*) was thus diversified into a plurality of habitus.

7. III, 11, 1.

8. Although (II-II, 174, 5, ad 3) the gift of prophecy was possessed by Christ only *insofar as He was viator.* In the view of St. Thomas, it is according as Christ was viator, and according as His infused science, received by right of comprehensor (III, 11, 2), illuminated also the viator, that this infused science was prophetic during His earthly life.

Elsewhere St. Thomas teaches (II-II, 171, 2) that the gift of prophecy is not a habitus. Let us understand (it is an explanation that I propose) that it is thus in the common human condition, but that in Him who was not *purus homo* the gift of prophecy was a habitus.

scious fully divinized and the sphere of consciousness, he regarded the infused science of Christ as relating entirely to the privileges of comprehensor (all the *species* of the one or the other of which the habitus of this science could use when it passed to the act at the wish of the will found themselves, therefore, from the very first infused in the soul), and it is this infused science of comprehensor which, for Him, found itself in Christ under a mode connatural to the human soul and illuminated also the viator. This is why he tells us still, and in the most insistent manner, that, through this infused science fully received from the beginning, and excluding the possibility of growing,[9] Christ, in His consciousness of viator, has known *omnia, all things* absolutely (III, q. 11, a. 1), including *omnia singularia praeterita, praesentia et futura* (*ibid.,* ad 3).

Behold therefore the Infant Jesus, from His birth, —nay, from the instant when His soul was created, —behold the infant Jesus in state of knowing at His wish in His consciousness of child *all things,* and to a degree of unsurpassable perfection, from the womb of Mary and from the cradle.

St. Thomas would have perhaps replied that it is the will to exercise in act this infused habitus which was lacking in the Child Jesus in the womb of His mother and in the cradle. The fact

9. St. Thomas admits no doubt that the outward effects or manifestations, the works produced went on increasing, in the case of the infused science of Christ as in that of His grace, but he holds that in itself the infused science of Christ (just as His grace) could not grow, *"habitus scientiae infusae in eo non est augmentatus: cum a principio plenarie sibi sit omnis scientia infusa"* (III, 12, 2). Christ had, therefore, in this view, received from the very first, —from the creation of His soul, —all the *species infusae* which He used at His will when He caused to pass, on one subject or the other, the habitus of His infused science to the exercise in act.

remains that such a proximate power to know all things, such a habitus of science totally infused from the creation of His soul seems to me, *in regard to Christ, child or adult, taken insofar as viator,* and in the exercise of that *conscious thought* in which He shared the common human condition, decidedly incompatible with the "mode connatural to the human soul" which St. Thomas admits for the infused science, and with the exigencies of *verus homo.*

THE INFUSED SCIENCE OF CHRIST ALSO FOUND ITSELF UNDER TWO DIFFERENT STATES IN THE HEAVEN OF HIS SOUL AND IN THE HERE-BELOW OF HIS SOUL

19. In the view which I am proposing, the infused science of Christ found itself in Him, like grace and like charity (and like the gifts of the Holy Spirit, which formed part of it) under the two *states* which we have distinguished:[10] state of final consum-

10. I recall here the essential point of the idea which I am proposing and which one can formulate thus: during the earthly pilgrimage of Jesus, the soul of the latter, and the whole universe of His interior life and of His thought, was simultaneously under two different regimes or states. The first regime, or state, was that which, in the already celestial and divinized supraconscious of the spirit, in the *heaven of the soul* of Christ, suited the man Jesus insofar precisely as blessed above every creature and as Saviour of the human race, in possession therefore, already, of the supreme End, of the accession to which He is *cause* for all the saved (cf. *Sum. Theol.,* III, 9, 2), and living already *divinely.* The second regime, or state, was that which, in the world of *consciousness* (in the usual sense of this word) centered on reason, or in the here-below of the soul of Christ, suited the Man Jesus, insofar precisely as living, acting, and suffering here on earth *humanly,* or *secundum modum connaturalem homini,* according to the human mode connatural to the *animal rationale* in its existence here on earth.

mation (in the divinized supraconsciousness of Christ, or His psychism already celestial) and state of way (in His psychism and His consciousness of man like us).

In the sphere of the divinized supraconsciousness (where Christ was *perfectus comprehensor*), it embraced *all things* absolutely, yes, —in this I am entirely of St. Thomas's opinion; for there, it is of the same infused science which Jesus will enjoy in Heaven that it was already a question: but, I insist, in a state totally unattainable to the consciousness. During the earthly life of Christ, His infused science, taken according as it found itself, in the sphere of the divinized supraconsciousness, under the state of final consummation, —was strictly *incommunicable.* For in the sphere in question, which was that where reigned the Beatific Vision (a Beatific Vision which did not invade and did not glorify the entire soul, and did not replace the reason as immediate rule of the actions of the soul, in short which created in the heights of the soul a sort of closed heaven), all that which was seized behind the veil was perfectly luminous and at the same time perfectly incommunicable, since entirely *supraconscious.*

In order that Christ as viator might express to Himself, *say* to Himself, in His consciousness of man like unto us, His infused science (caused in His soul *ex unione ad Verbum,* III, 12, 2, ad 3), it was necessary that this infused science not find itself only in the supraconscious paradise of the soul of Christ; it was necessary also that, in proportion as the sphere of the consciousness or of the here-below of the soul of Christ forms itself, His infused science hold sway in this other sphere, where it is subject to the regime *connatural to the human soul* and where, in order to translate into a properly human lexicon its infused ideative forms, more angelic than human, it could *use instrumentally concepts formed under the light of the agent intellect,* and without which we cannot speak to ourselves. Is it not thus only that in the use that Christ has made of it here on earth it could, as St. Thomas wishes, be *collativa et discursiva*,[11] proceed discursively and by mode of rational linking? In short, it was necessary that it exist also, in order that Christ could make use of it during His earthly life, *in the sphere of the here-below of the soul of Christ,* where, at the same stroke, it found itself *under the state of way.* Thus therefore, and because the very fact that it was due to ideative forms (infused) rendered possible its exercise in the conditions which I have just indicated, the infused science of Christ was rendered, —in that sphere, —*communicable* (that which is absolutely impossible to the Beatific Vision).

It is this infused science existing *under the state of way* that I would like now to consider.

It is necessary to say, in my view, —not only that the infused science held sway in the sphere of the here-below of the soul of Christ (where it found itself under the state of way, and diversified into a plurality of habitus)[12] only in proportion as this sphere

11. *Sum. Theol.,* III, 11, 3. St. Thomas tells us himself that if, according to that which it received *a causa influente,* the infused science of Christ was a great deal more excellent than that of the angels, on the other hand, however, *secundum id quod habuit* [here on earth] *ex subjecto recipiente,* "*scientia indita animae Christi est infra scientiam angelicam; scilicet: quantum ad modum cognoscendi, qui est* per conversionem ad phantasmata, *et per collationem et discursum*" (III, 11, 4).

12. *Scientia indita Christi fuit distincta secundum diversos habitus (Sum. Theol.,* III, 11, 6). This is enough to permit one to say, in the recasting that I am proposing, that the habitus proper to the infused science such as it was in the paradise of the soul of Christ (where it was infinite in its order) was *another habitus* (cf. p. 91, note 6) than those through which it exercised itself in the here-below of the latter. According to my view, the case of the infused science is thus different from that of charity, undivided habitus which found itself, in the paradise and in the here-below of the soul of Christ, under two different states of existence (and hence of operation).

itself took shape, at the same time as there developed in the child the exercise of intelligence and of reason, —but that in this sphere of the here-below of the soul of Christ it grew (just as the grace and the charity) and did not cease to grow during His whole earthly life.[13] And at each moment of this development [14] it extended itself to all that which Jesus had need to know *at that moment* (I mean at that period of His progress in age and in wisdom). It is only after His death on the Cross [15] that He made

13. To say that in the here-below of the soul of Christ the habitus of His infused science grew unceasingly, is to say that they were infused, just as the *species* which they used, in a measure more and more ample and abundant; and it is to say also that—full or infinite in the heaven of the soul, —it remained finite in the here-below of the latter.

In His speech on the great tribulation and the coming of the Son of Man in glory, Jesus has said: "But of that day or hour no one knows, neither the angels in heaven, nor the Son, but the Father only" (Mk. 13, 32; Matt. 24, 36). It is necessary to understand: although *in the Heaven of His soul* Christ knew this day through the Vision and through an infinite infused science, but *altogether supraconscious and incommunicable,* He did not know it *in the here-below of His soul,* where His infused science radiated in His consciousness and was communicable, but was received only progressively and *was not infinite.*

14. It did not increase by reason of His acts, as did the charity (cf. above, Section 17), but by reason of the growing need which Christ had to make use of it in proportion as He grew in age. Likewise, if after the death on the Cross the infused science of Christ became infinite in its order, it is not that the infused science at the state of way has increased to the point of passing the threshold of the infinite and of being identified with the infused science proper to the comprehensor, it is that at the moment of the death of Christ the finite (and increasing) infused science proper to the state of way has yielded place to the infused science at the state of final consummation which ceased to be enclosed in the supraconscious paradise of the soul, and was about to exercise itself fully for eternity (see further on, Section 31).

15. I have already remarked (p. 90, note 2) that the infused science of Christ (such as it was in the paradise of His soul) continued to exist and to exercise itself in Heaven, where it was not rendered superfluous by the Vision. It is in making use of it that Christ exercises concerning all things

practical use of the infused science *infinite* in its order that He had possessed on earth in the paradise of His soul,—and which henceforth reigns in act in His whole soul, causing Him to know explicitly *all things,* —in order to "manage," if I may say, or "administer" until the last judgment, —and in the centuries of centuries, —the work of salvation of the human race (accomplished by Him on the Cross on Good Friday, and continued in time, as to its application, by the Church) and in order to exercise His universal lordship. It is only in Heaven that His infused science [16] gives Him the fully and gloriously manageable knowledge of the infinity of created detail which is required for this, so that He can express to Himself, in using species infused by suprahuman mode, and express to the angels, His ministers, in proportion as they receive His commands, all this created infinite which He knows in a more sublime manner in His Beatific Vision (the latter being, in Heaven as it was for Him on earth, absolutely ineffable and inexpressible by any created *species,* even in that which concerns the creatures which it causes to see in God, for its absolute unity and indivisibility, which stem from the actuation of the intellect by the divine essence itself, exclude all possibility of parcelling out, —it is an eternal flash of which absolutely nothing can be said through an idea).

---

here on earth, and all men, His functions of King and of Judge. The Beatific Vision is not something which a created intellect can *use;* it is the immediate rule of the whole action of the glorious Christ, because everything in His soul bathes in the light of the Vision. But it is not of it that the glorious Christ can *make use* in order to formulate mentally decrees, command His angels and bear judgments. His infinite infused science is necessary to the exercise of His universal lordship.

16. St. Thomas (after St. Paul, 1 Cor. 13, 8) teaches that the gift of prophecy will cease in Heaven (II-II, q. 174, a. 5). But the infused science of Christ was prophetic only by reason of His state of viator (cf. III, 7, 8).

THE EVIDENCE OF THE BEATIFIC VISION WAS PARTICIPATED IN BY THE INFUSED SCIENCE OF CHRIST

20. Unlike prophecy, which, when it entails evidence, entails evidence only *in attestante,* the infused science of Jesus entailed *intrinsic evidence* of the truth known itself. Moreover, this intrinsic evidence was a *participation of the very evidence of the vision.* There is here a point of major importance to be elucidated.

To say that the infused science was in the soul of Christ under two different states, the one of consummated, immutable, and eternal perfection, in the paradise of the soul, the other of growth in perfection in the here-below of the latter, is to say that the infused ideative forms (*species infusae*) which it received in these two states differed in perfection; those of the paradise of the soul were of consummated perfection, those of the here-below of the soul were of increasing perfection (that is to say, infused in a manner more and more abundantly illuminating). Let us try to see this more closely.

In every *purus homo,* in all of us others, —let us say, if you will, in Thomas Aquinas for instance, —the idea of the Trinity or that of the resurrection from the dead which we had at the age of six, in learning our catechism (the idea that the little Thomas had at that age), was not the same as the idea which we will have at adult age (that Thomas Aquinas had when he wrote the *Summa*). Supposing (sheer imaginary hypothesis) that instead of acquired ideas these ideas had been infused ideas, the infused science received by us would have therefore grown little by little: the infused idea which it would have used in the child of six years would have been less perfect than that which it would have used in the man of thirty years. It would not have been less *true,* less pure, in itself, of all error, —(although, I do not know, grafted also perhaps with parasitic imageries, in themselves illusory, which are natural to childhood, at least in the *purus homo*).

Well, let us seek in this example an imaginary analogy in order to aid us in thinking of the case of the *verus sed non purus homo,* in that which concerns in particular that itself which Jesus had come in order to reveal, and which we must especially consider here, —the divine mysteries. In the Child Jesus of six years (and to whom Mary taught as to a child holy truths which He knew under a better mode through His infused ideas still at the measure of childhood,[17] and infinitely better than she in the supraconscious of His soul) the ideative form which His infused science *growing in the here-below of His soul* used was as *true* as the infused ideative form informing, in the paradise of His soul, His infused science at the state of consummated perfection. As *true* (pure of all error), in its intact nature of intuitional intelligible form, as the ideative form received by the infused science in the paradise of the soul of Christ, it was *less perfect,* because *its content of knowledge was less rich.* And all along the life of Jesus this content of knowledge brought by the ideative forms proper to His infused science in the here-below of His soul grew in richness and in perfection.

All this posited, let us recall now that the Beatific Vision, where

17. Suppose (that which appears normal to me) that in the little Child Jesus these infused ideas, absolutely independent in themselves of the phantasms from which are drawn the acquired ideas, were surrounded by the imageries natural to childhood, their intuitive brilliance, due to their participation in the evidence of the Vision, dispelled from these imageries all illusory signification.

it is the divine essence itself which actuates the intellect (angelic or human) in the manner of a *species impressa,* causes this intellect to see not only the abyss of the uncreated Being, but also the things known by the latter, —and not only according to the being which they have eternally in the Word, but also according to the being which they have in their own nature,[18] and in their proper duration, which is time.

The infused science, even in the state of consummated perfection which it had in the paradise of the soul of Christ, could clearly not attain to the transcendent and, if I may say, "in excess" perfection of His Beatific Vision, since it was a knowledge through created ideative forms. Through His infused *species* taken according to their proper nature, this infused science was nevertheless capable of knowing by created mode, —with a consummated perfection in the paradise of the soul of Christ, with an increasing perfection in the here-below of this science, —the things hidden in God and in the uncreated science, I do not say according to *that which* they are in their essence,[19] I say according to *that they are*[20] in actual fact (and can be known analogically), —in other words, the truths hidden in God which the Beatific Vision caused Christ to know in a divine (*in Verbo*) and infinitely superior manner.[21] It is necessary, however, to go much further. For in the

18. *Secundum quod cognoscunt esse rerum quod habent in propria natura, videndo Verbum. Sum. Theol.,* I, 50, 7.

19. Question *quid est,* or *quomodo est,* in Scholastic terminology: let us say, question of *the essence of.* (To know the "that which" *in itself.*)

20. Question *an est.* Let us say: question of the *fact that.* (It is to know also the *that which,* but under the veil of the created analogates.)

21. Cf. John of Saint Thomas, *Curs. theol.,* Vivès, t. VIII, disp. 13, a. 1. —John of Saint Thomas explains there that through His infused science Christ knew *omnia illa quae per revelationem divinam hominibus innotescunt,* —cf. *Sum. Theol.,* III, 11, 1, —and consequently the Trinity

infused science at the state of increasing perfection as in the infused science at the state of consummated perfection, the knowledge due to the infused *species* taken according to their proper
nature was of itself, as I have just said, an intellectual knowledge
through evidence, but moreover, and it is this that matters above
all, this knowledge was *ruled,* and *immediately* ruled, by the
Beatific Vision which existed in the heaven of the soul of Christ.

What does this mean? It was a question there of a privilege of
Christ, due to the mission for which He had come, —*to reveal
divinely* the mysteries of grace hidden in God. His vision of
God, —the *actuation of His intellect by the divine essence itself,
in the light of glory,* —is the rule which God *used as instrument*
in order to produce the infused science, its habitus and its *species,*
as well *in the here-below* as *in the paradise* of this same intellect.
The effect proper to the use of this instrument: the divine Vision
illuminating the intellect of Christ, by the first Cause in order to
produce the infused *species* in this same intellect, was therefore,
—not indeed to cause to pass into the infused science of Christ
the objective content itself, indivisibly and ineffably seized, of

---

quoad an est (n. 6), and the hypostatic union *in individuo et secundum
omnes circumstantias suas, secundum quas de facto terminata est ad
hypostasim Verbi, et non ad aliam Personam* (n. 16). *Eo modo cognovit
hanc unionem per speciem infusam,* he writes further (no. 17), *quo nos
per fidem illam credimus.* And again: *Satis absurdum est quod per scientiam infusam, QUA CHRISTUS CONSTITUTUS EST UNIVERSUS
DOCTOR ANGELORUM ET HOMINUM, non possit instruere aliquem
in articulis fidei* (no. 9).

The views advanced by John of Saint Thomas in this article go in the
same direction as the assertions here proposed, which add to them, nevertheless, an indispensable consideration in my opinion, that of the instrumental use made by God of the intellect of Christ insofar as actuated by
the divine essence itself (His Beatific Vision) in order to produce in this
same intellect the *species* of the infused science.

the Beatific Vision, nor to transmit to it the proper light of the latter, which is the *lumen gloriae,* —but to elevate the evidence of which the infused *species* are, in themselves, bearers to *participate* in the evidence of the Vision; in other words, it was to cause to see the objective content of the *species* in question with an evidence which is a *participation of the divine evidence of the Vision,*[22] — and with a divinely absolute certitude as invincible as that of which the intellect is possessed in the Vision. Thus the light through which these infused *species* attained their object was, consequently, a *participation* in the light of the Vision.

One can therefore say, if one wishes, but in a manner which needs to be well understood, that an *influx of intellectual light*[23] stemming from the Vision was communicated to the infused science of Christ, and that something of that which He knew through the Vision in His divinized supraconsciousness was communicated to the sphere of the consciousness, —not, indeed, ac-

---

22. To say that the evidence of the infused science of Christ was an evidence *participated of His Vision,* is certainly not to say that it was an evidence *divine in itself* (uncreated) like that of the Vision! It is to say that it was an evidence *divine by participation,* bringing to the mind a certitude *divine by participation.* It was due to a created light divinely superelevated by grace, and which caused to participate in the divine or uncreated evidence of the Beatific Vision just as grace causes to participate in the divine or uncreated nature of the Most High. It was a radiance, an evidence divine by participation, proper to the objective content of the *species* of the infused science of Christ in the here-below of His soul as in the paradise of the latter, and which gave Him in the here-below of His soul the certitude divine by participation required by His mission of Revealer.

The case of the infused science is thus, in my view, the only case where something in the here-below of the soul of Christ was immediately ruled by His Beatific Vision, because produced by God *using the latter as instrument.*

23. I employ here, in transposing it, an expression which St. Thomas uses with respect to the gift of prophecy (II-II, 173, 2).

cording as the ineffable and indivisible *content* of the science of Vision would have been parcelled out in communicable *species* and in conscious ideas, but according as the infused science was the *exchange agency* thanks to which the divine gold of the Vision was changed into the coin of the expressible and communicable *species*.[24]

And that which the latter transmitted was the divine Truth which in His Beatific Vision Christ saw in itself—as giving itself to be known by itself—at the very highest part of the heaven of His soul, and of which, thanks to the ideative forms of the infused science such as it found itself in the here-below of His soul, something was rendered accessible to men, through the means of the concepts (*verba mentis*) in which the intellect of Christ uttered within itself that which it saw through this infused science, and of the rational discursus,[25] and of the "conversion towards images," and of the comparisons and parables, and of all the concrete and sensible illustrations supplied by the experimental science. All this marvellous effusion of human thought and of human word transmitted a knowledge divinely true, divinely certain, and divinely infallible, because it expressed an infused science which—while bearing (like faith in us) not on the *essence,* seen by the Vision only, of the mysteries hidden in God (*that which* they are

24. The *species* of the infused science are expressible and communicable of themselves when they are employed according to the mode of the pure spirits. But when they are employed according to the human mode it is only in using instrumentally concepts formed by abstraction, under the light of the agent intellect (cf. above, p. 94–95) that they can express themselves and speak themselves. It is the case which we have to consider when we speak of Christ as viator.

25. This science, says St. Thomas, was discursive, *discursiva vel collativa,* not as regards the manner of acquiring it (since it was infused), but *as regards the use* which Christ made of it. "*Poterat enim ex uno aliud concludere, sicut sibi placebat*" (III, 11, 3).

in themselves), but only on *the fact that* they are,[26] —*participated*, in order to cause to see these things properly divine, *in the evidence of the Vision,* and possessed the sovereign authority conferred by it. When it is a question of the mystery of the deity, there is no middle ground between the evidence of the Beatific Vision and theological faith; in other words, there is only one evidence possible with regard to the diety, —that of the vision: this evidence however can be *participated.* Not having theological faith, it is through the *evidence*—but *participated*—of the *science of Beatific Vision* that the infused science of Christ caused Him to know the divine things, —His own divinity, His own procession from the Father, His Incarnation, His redemptive Mission, the unity in nature of the three divine Persons, the procession of the Holy Spirit, in short, all the divine Inaccessible which He had to reveal, to "tell" to men, —*ipse enarravit.*

It is absurd to imagine that Christ would have had like us theological faith. He had come—He, the Incarnate Word, the God made Man—in order *to reveal divinely* the truths and the mysteries on which this faith lives, and to which it adheres on the testimony and the teaching of *God revealing,* or of the subsisting Truth itself making itself known. Jesus did not *believe,* —He *knew.* He did not have theological faith, He had the *knowledge* to which this faith is suspended. Does this mean that it is *His Beatific Vision itself* which He communicated in His teaching? No, if it is a question of the content of the Beatific Vision such as it is exchanged into coin—at least in that which concerns the transmitted revealed—by the infused science, which itself participates in the evidence of the Vision.

It seems to me that one understands better thus this great text

---

26. And on *that which* they are, but thanks only to the analogy of proper proportionality. Cf. *The Degrees of Knowledge,* new translation, Appendix III.

from the Gospel of St. John: "'Who art thou?' Jesus said to them: 'the Beginning, I who speak with you.[27] I have many things to speak and to judge concerning you; but he who sent me is true, and the things that I heard from him, these I speak in the world, *et ego quae audivi ab eo, haec loquor in mundo.*' And they did not understand that he was speaking to them about the Father. Jesus therefore said to them, 'When you have lifted up [on the Cross] the Son of Man, then you will know that *I am*,[28] and that of myself I do nothing: but that which I have learned from my Father, it is this that I speak, *sicut docuit me Pater, haec loquor*."

In this text (Jn., 8, 25–29) He has not said: that which I have seen close by the Father; He has said: *that which I have learned from the Father.* Learned, how? *Through the infused science,* itself participating in the evidence of the Vision, which in the here-below of His soul permitted Him to *say to Himself,* and to *say to men,* something of that which He saw in the Vision (but which, insofar as seen in the Vision, remained, of itself, ineffable). Christ revealing has Himself learned from the Father [29] that which He reveals to us, but He did not learn it by *listening*

---

27. τὴν ἀρχὴν ὅ τι καὶ λαλῶ ὑμῖν (8, 25). This text is among the most difficult, and modern translators translate it otherwise. The Jerusalem Bible translates: "What I have told you from the outset," and remarks in a footnote that "the Vulgate translation is grammatically impossible." Perhaps; and I have indeed for the more rigorous precisions which exegesis provides us the gratitude which is due to them (see further on, p. 111, note 43). I ask nevertheless the permission to prefer it, because it agrees in a very striking manner with the "Before Abraham came to be, *I am*" of 8, 58, and because it seems to me that if, in reality, the accusative τὴν ἀρχὴν is then an error in grammar, one can still understand before it, not "I am," but something such as "you see" or "you have before you," [You have before you] *the Beginning, this is that which I tell you.*

28. In referring to the Semitic substitute *ego eimi,* Abbé Feuillet, together with other contemporary exegetes, translates here (8, 28): "then you will know that *it is I,*" cf. further on, p. 111, note 43.

29. Or, as it is said four lines above in the same text, "heard" from the Father (8, 26). The voice of the Father was the *science given* by Him.

105

through faith, He learned it by *seeing through the science* immediately received from God (*infused science*).

I am not forgetting that elsewhere He has said also: "Amen, amen, I say to thee, we speak of what we know, and we bear witness to *what we have* SEEN; and our witness you do not receive"; [30] "I speak *what I have* SEEN with the Father"; [31] "He who comes from heaven . . . bears witness to that which he has SEEN and HEARD"; [32] "Not that anyone has seen the Father except him who is from God, *he has* SEEN *the Father.*" [33] In all these texts, he who is concerned is *this man who speaks to you at this moment.* In affirming *that He has seen* the Father, and that He speaks *that which He has seen* with the Father, Jesus renders testimony to the *science of Vision* which He has here on earth as have in Heaven "the angels who see the face of the Father," [34] and as will have in Heaven "those who are pure of heart." [35] And in affirming that He bears witness to that which He has seen and *heard,* or to that which He *has learned from the Father,*[36] He renders testimony to His *infused science,* received by reason of the Vision and by means of the Vision, and through which *He reveals to us,* translated into concepts, and into words of our language, things which in the Vision are seen under incommunicable mode. This is how I understand the sublime abridgment of the Prologue of John: "No one has at any time *seen* God. The only-begotten Son, who is in the bosom of the Father, he has revealed him." [37]

30. Jn. 3, 11.
31. Jn. 8, 38.
32. Jn. 3, 32.
33. Jn. 6, 46.
34. Matt. 18, 10.
35. Matt. 5, 8.
36. Cf. above, p. 105 (Jn. 8, 29).
37. Jn. 1, 18.

THE KNOWLEDGE THAT JESUS HAD OF HIS DIVINITY

21. It seems clear to me that that which mattered the most, and in a manner absolutely primordial, in the infused science such as it found itself in the soul of Christ, was the knowledge that it gave Him *of His divinity.*

In fact, He knew certainly, and in the most perfect manner, His divinity through the Beatific Vision, but this Vision was shut up in the supraconscious paradise of His soul, and, moreover, it was by essence absolutely simple and absolutely *inexpressible* in any idea. It is not, therefore, through the Vision that He could know in the sphere of the here-below of His soul, and know so as to express it to Himself, that He was God. It is on the infused science, itself participating in the evidence of the Vision, that depends this knowledge that Christ as viator had of His divinity (and, at the same time, of His mission).

Insofar as comprehensor, He knew Himself God through the Vision, *in seeing the divine essence and His own divine Person and the Father with whom He is one:* science supremely perfect (perfect "to excess") and perpetually in act, even during sleep (but inaccessible to the consciousness). Insofar as viator, He knew Himself God *through His infused science,* —finite and increasing under the state of way, but which under this state (in the here-below of the soul of Christ) *participated in the evidence of the Beatific Vision* in the same manner and for the same reason as in the heaven of the soul proper to the comprehensor. And it is this participated evidence of the Vision which gave to the infused science of the Son of God *viator* a *divinely* sovereign *certitude* with regard to all that which it knew, and especially with regard to the very divinity of Jesus.

107

This infused science was certainly very different from the Beatific Vision, —it was procured through intelligible *species* or ideative forms, not through the divine essence actuating immediately the intellect, —but these intelligible *species*, divinely illumined by their participation in the evidence of the Beatific Vision, caused Him to *see*, in the here-below as in the heaven of His soul, and with a divinely sovereign certitude, *that He was* the Word Incarnate, essentially one with the Father. (To see *God* was the affair of His Beatific Vision; to see *that He was God*, that of His infused science).

And in the sphere of the consciousness, or of the here-below of His soul, where His infused science expressed itself in interior words of human mode, He could say to Himself, He knew with conceptual and communicable science, that He was God. This knowledge of His own divinity He had already in germ as soon as He was old enough to speak to Himself,[38] —in the manner, no doubt, still scarcely conscious proper to early childhood, but in order to become already perfect or complete at the "age of reason," and to continue to grow in richness and in perfection all through His life.

THE KNOWLEDGE THAT JESUS HAD OF HIS MISSION

22. That which I have just said of the knowledge that He had of His divinity, it is necessary to say also of that which He had of His mission, as also of that which He had of all the mysteries which He had come in order to reveal.

The mission of Jesus included a multitude of concordant aspects of a marvellous richness: He had come in order to render testimony to the Truth, —in order to reveal the mysteries of grace

38. Cf. further on, p. 119–120.

and of love hidden in God, —in order to glorify the Father, —in order to announce the glad tidings of the Kingdom of God, and to preach the Gospel to the poor, —in order to found His Church, —He had come in order to save the world, in order to save everything in the supreme humiliation of the scorn which He would suffer, and of the persecution which was His lot as it will be that of His friends, and of the ignominy of the torment in which He accomplished the supreme sacrifice, He had come in order to be immolated on the Cross and in order to rise again on the third day, and then to enter into the glory reserved for Him who by right of nature was King, and in order to bring with Him humanity redeemed and sanctified by Him into the glory of the sons of God by participation, living with eternal life with the three divine Persons.

It is not surprising that according to the moments and the circumstances He should have let men see now one, now another of the aspects of this mission; one can think that to the knowledge which He had of it through His infused science participating in the evidence of His Vision, there came to join themselves in the course of His life many truths *perceived,* felt in His flesh as in His spirit by His experience of man (in other words, which He possessed from His "experimental science"). It is foolish to imagine [39]

39. In the manner of certain authors who think, for example, that under the experience of the failures met with by His preaching Jesus has passed, in the consciousness of His mission, from an ideal and more or less chimerical view to a view finally real, and acceded thus to a "messianic consciousness" which was lacking to Him at first, —or that He understood that He had to go to the Cross only after the Jewish people had refused His message, so that He formed for Himself then of the Kingdom of God another idea than that which He had at the beginning of His ministry, —or that He was certain only after the episode of the Transfiguration, and the revelation which it brought to Him, of a destiny which He had begun to feel only at the moment of His failure in Galilee. Perspicacious explainers! However ingenious one may be (and modest), it would be necessary, nevertheless, to know first OF WHOM one is speaking, —this

that He Himself would have been able to form for Himself an idea of His mission which would have changed with time, and would have depended on the accidents to which every lofty human purpose is exposed, as if He had been but a poor great enlightened one seeking His way through the hostility of established people and the prejudices of the mass, and in the midst of the disheartening tribulations of earthly existence. He knew all the aspects of His mission in a manner divinely true and divinely certain, of which the perfection, i.e. the richness in objective content, did not cease to grow until the end.

---

seems to be a good method for the psychologist-historian as well as for everybody.

I take the liberty of adding here a few remarks with reference to the Gospels of the Infancy, and to that which one hears said today concerning them in certain milieux where, without having reflected either on the ways of man or on those of God, one makes the most naïve use of a notion such as that of literary genres, which, like every learned notion, demands to be intelligently applied. On one hand, there is in man, with respect to the events of life, *types of mental expectation* ("prospective images," if one wishes so to speak) which, being in accordance with the instinct of the heart and of reason, are found all through the ages of humanity. On the other hand, there is a language of events just as there is a language of words, and it is clear that in order to make oneself understood by someone it is necessary to speak his language. This is apparently the custom of God, —who would hardly have a chance of being understood by men if in order to speak to them He did not consent to employ their vocabulary.

It is consistent with a natural instinct of the heart and of the reason to expect that the birth of a predestined child will be accompanied by providential signs. If God wishes to make man understand that a certain child is not only a predestined child, but His own Son sent among us, He will take care to surround His birth with such providential signs, —because it is here the "language of events" which is spontaneously intelligible to man: so much the better (except for the foolish Doctors) if man has gone in advance in the course of his history, and surrounded with analogous signs—more or less imaginary this time—, the birth of the heroes of his mythologies, or that of inspired masters whom he has held (with good reason, I readily believe) as great predestined ones. It was there, at the heart of our race, a preparation for the divine ways.

THE REVELATION BY JESUS OF THE
MYSTERIES OF GRACE HIDDEN IN GOD

23. He has come to bring fire upon the earth,[40] because He is the Truth.[41] The mysteries which He revealed, —*docens sicut potestatem habens,*[42]—He knew them also in a manner divinely true, divinely certain, and divinely evident, through His infused science which participated in the evidence of His Vision.

All the truths which refer to His mission of Saviour and of Redeemer, He has taught Himself, they are set down in the Gospels. Jesus has taught us that before Abraham was, *He is*[43];

40. Lk. 12, 49.
41. Jn. 14, 6.
42. Matt. 7, 29.
43. "Before Abraham came to be, *I am.*" Jn. 8, 58. (Cf. Jn. 17, 5: "And now do thou, Father, glorify me with thyself, with the glory that I had with thee before the world existed.")
I am happy to find confirmation, by an exegete of such high value as Abbé André Feuillet, of the translation of the text of Jn. 8, 58 such as I have given it here. Cf. André Feuillet, "Les *Ego eimi* christologiques du quatrième Évangile," *Recherches de Science religieuse,* January-March 1966, p. 18. In this study the author insists in a decisive manner (*ibid.,* April-June 1966, pp. 238-240) on a point that every Christian should hold to be indubitable, and which is central in the present book, but which appears today "hardly credible" to many fickle minds, —namely, the consciousness that Christ had of His divinity.
I note that for another text of the Gospel of St. John, which I have cited above (p. 105, Jn. 8, 25), Abbé Feuillet adopts the translation: "I am from the beginning (that is to say, since always) that which I tell you," and rejects, as one does generally today, the version of the Vulgate, to which go my preferences. The latter certainly count for little in face of his competence. Nevertheless, I take the liberty, I who am not an exegete but a philosopher, to remain attached to the Vulgate, for the very simple reason (perhaps excessively simple, but does one ever know?) that St. Jerome knew Greek as well as we. Moreover, Abbé Feuillet brings us on

111

that He is the Son of God,[44] the only-begotten [45] Son who will sit at the right hand of God; [46] that all that the Father has is His,[47] that He and the Father are one,[48] and one with them the Spirit of Truth, the Paraclete who proceeds from the Father [49] and whom the Son will send us; [50] that He has come forth from the Father in order to come into the world,[51] and has become the Son of Man [52] by descending into flesh; that He, the author of life,[53] has suffered the death on the Cross (His "baptism," the waiting for which consumed Him)[54] in order to deliver us from the sins of the world [55] and to render us through His Resurrection participants of His glory; [56] that He is the Resurrection and the Life; [57] that all power has been given to Him in Heaven and on earth,[58] and that He will come in His majesty to judge the world and to separate the just from those who have not loved, the latter

---

this text (as on 8, 24 and 8, 28, where he translates ἐγώ εἰμι by "it is I": *ibid.,* March-April 1966, p. 17) a commentary of great depth and of great truth. Yes, Jesus has wished to give an enigmatic form to certain affirmations too high for the men who heard them (and who had not yet received the Holy Spirit), "He leaves to future history the care of interpreting the obscure words which He utters."

44. Lk. 22, 70; 10, 22. Cf. Matt. 26, 63-64; Mk. 14, 61-62; Jn. 19, 7.
45. Jn. 3, 16-18.
46. Matt. 26, 64; Mk. 14, 62; Lk. 22, 69.
47. Jn. 16, 15.
48. Jn. 10, 30. (Cf. 10, 38; 17, 21-22.)
49. Jn. 15, 26.
50. Lk. 24, 49.
51. Jn. 16, 27.
52. Matt. 8, 20; 9, 6, etc.
53. Acts 3, 15.
54. *"Quomodo coarctor usquedum perficiatur."* Lk. 12, 50.
55. Jn. 1, 29.
56. Jn. 17, 10.
57. Jn. 11, 25.
58. Matt. 28, 18.

going into the everlasting fire prepared for the devil and his angels, the former, the blessed of His Father, into everlasting life, into the Kingdom prepared for them from the foundation of the world; [59] that there is but one baptism—in the name of the Father, and of the Son, and of the Holy Spirit [60]—for the remission of sins, and but one Church built upon the rock that is Peter; [61] that everything on earth is ordered to the life of the world to come [62] and of that Paradise into which the good thief entered with Him; that His Kingdom is not of this world; [63] that the Providence of God holds in its hand all beings and all events great and small; [64] that evil comes from the Enemy,[65] the Father of Lies; [66] and that God is Love; [67] and that He, Jesus, is the living bread come down from Heaven.[68]

"No one has at any time seen God. The only-begotten Son, who is in the bosom of the Father, He has revealed Him." [69] At the heart of the Gospel He has put this saying: "God is spirit, and they who worship him must worship in spirit and in truth." [70]

59. Matt. 25, 31-46.
60. Matt. 28, 19.
61. Matt. 16, 18.
62. Matt. 6, 19-21; Lk. 12, 16-32.
63. Jn. 18, 36.
64. Matt. 10, 29-31.
65. Cf. Matt. 13, 25-28.
66. Jn. 8, 44. —The Father of Lies: he engenders nothingness in being (the escape into nothingness in the freedom of the will), because *"there is no truth* in him (*Ibid.*); "when he tells a lie *he speaks from his very nature"* (*Ibid*).
67. The phrase is from St. John (I, 4, 8); but Jesus had said it equivalently (Matt. 5, 44-46; 7, 7-12; Lk. 6, 35; 11, 11-13).
68. Jn. 6, 50-51.
69. Jn. 1, 18. —Instead of "the only-begotten Son," one reads in two manuscripts (Sinaiticus, Vaticanus): "a God only-begotten Son."
70. Jn. 4, 24.

The Gospel is turned entirely towards *the mystery of God,* —to which man is assumed.[71]

2. *Additional Questions*

THE CONSCIOUSNESS OF CHRIST AS VIATOR

24. The knowledge that Christ, insofar as viator, had of His divinity and of His mission and of the other supernatural truths hidden in the glory of God, was the highest knowledge possible of infused science.

As I have indicated above, the knowledge, through infused science, of His own divinity, developed during the childhood of Jesus probably very quickly, indeed before He was able to translate it for Himself into concepts and to express it to Himself, because of the natural intuitivity of the child. It is necessary to say as much of the consciousness that the Saviour had of Himself.

I have spoken until now of the infused science of Christ, that is to say, of an infused knowledge of a nature *purely intellectual* or *principally intellectual.*

The question of the *consciousness* that Christ had of His divinity is a different question. In general, St. Thomas, when he speaks of the knowledge that we have of ourselves, has never in view anything but the *intellectual intuition* or *grasp* that the soul would have or would not have of its own essence, and it is this intuition or intellectual grasp that He refuses to it. If it is a ques-

71. One perverts the Gospel and one belies the truth when one imagines it centered on *the wonders of Man* in the act of becoming God (although *man is dead,* as inform us the latest heirs, and intelligent ones, certainly, of the metaphysical discoveries of modern thought when it has read—and understood—Nietzsche).

tion of a purely intellectual knowledge, or of the informing of the intellect by an intelligible in act, the human soul grasps—by reflection on its acts—only its existence and the existence of the subject, not its essence.

The notion of *consciousness* does not appear explicitly in the text of St. Thomas and, as a matter of fact, it is a notion more modern. The word "consciousness" connotes a knowledge essentially *experimental* and *perceived* (by reversion on acts); this is an *obscure* knowledge and which of itself is inexpressible in concepts, —and which, of course, does not attain the essence of the soul. When it can express itself in concepts, it is by reflection on it of the conceptualizing intellect.

I have thus—and without ever perceiving my own essence—the obscure knowledge not only of my *existence* but of my *subjectivity,* knowledge in which connaturality plays an essential role (cf. *Existence and the Existent,* Ch. III). In such a way, for example, that by the obscure experience of my liberty, and of a life within me which transcends the bondage of the senses, I experience obscurely that I react as man to a given situation, even supposing that I have not yet formed the concept of man, and am therefore incapable of saying to myself that I am a man. But in actual fact, I have formed this concept of man by another route, in the exercise of my intellect turned naturally towards things, and as a concept abstracted from sensible experience by the agent intellect. And from the moment that this concept reflects back upon the obscurely perceived content of the consciousness, and from the moment that the latter recognizes that it coincides with its own obscure experience of subjectivity, my consciousness is able to say it to itself, I have explicitly (but thanks to the intervention of an intellectual knowledge of other origin) *consciousness of being a man.*

Well, it seems to me that one can, *mutatis mutandis,* apply these reflections to the case of the consciousness which the Lord had of Himself, in the here-below of His soul. Insofar as consciousness is a knowledge wholly experimental and felt, which of itself is obscure and inexpressible in concepts, I shall say that Christ had consciousness not only of His existence and not only of the fact that He was "someone," but also, —through the lived experience of His absolute impeccability, of His faultless wisdom, as also through the ineffable memory of that which He had experienced in prayer, —He had consciousness of the fact that He transcended the human condition, and that there was in Him something divine.[72] And from the moment that the perfectly clear purely intellectual knowledge, —furnished by the infused science, —that He was the Son of God, the Word Incarnate,

72. Is it necessary to add, with Father Diepen (*La Théologie de l'Emmanuel,* p. 217) that, through lived experience, each time that He acted, with a mysterious and total ontological *dependence,* Christ, not being conscious of any human *I* (being conscious, writes Father Diepen, "of the absence of the human *I*," —but is one conscious of an absence?) suspected already that the *I* from which proceeded all His acts was a divine *I?* I do not think so. For there is dependence, in the sense in which Father Diepen understood it, only with respect to *another,* —another *subject.* But there was in Christ only one single and unique subject, the divine *I.* And Christ did not, therefore, feel Himself more *dependent* in regard to it than we feel *dependent* on our human *I.* In short, all His human activity, including that of His free will, was the instrument of the divine Word (cf. *Sum Theol.,* III, 18, 1, ad 2), just as our activity is the instrument of our created person (although it did not emanate from the Word in the manner in which our activity emanates from our self), and the human consciousness of Jesus held the Word as His own *I* just as our consciousness holds our created person to be our own *I: Non mea voluntas, sed tua fiat* (Lk. 22, 42): "My will" (*voluntas ut natura,* specifies St. Thomas, III, 18, 5, will as desire of nature) "*my* will, it was that of the Word Incarnate insofar precisely as Incarnate, and insofar precisely as viator, and insofar precisely as having (in opposition to all His desires of nature *secundum quod erat homo*) to bear the sins of the world, and insofar as putting instrumentally into play the faculties of human nature hypostatically assumed.

116

reflected upon this content obscurely felt of consciousness—from that moment the consciousness of Christ, illuminating by this knowledge of infused science (which itself participated in the evidence of the Vision), the experience lived by it, extended (but thanks to the intervention of an intellectual knowledge of another order) even to the divinity of the Person of Christ. He had thus (thanks to His infused science) *consciousness* of Himself as of a *divine Person,* He had consciousness of being the Word Incarnate. Whereas at the same time He obviously had consciousness also— and in virtue of the same reflection of the infused science (as also this time, of the experimental science) on the obscure content of consciousness—that He was *man* as well, or that His *nature* was *human.*

Let us add that the reading of, and an incomparably profound meditation upon, the holy Scriptures had, on the side of experimental science,[73] certainly to integrate themselves also with that

73. St. Thomas has caused theology to take a decisive step forward in recognizing in the *Summa Theologica,* —that which, as he indicates himself (*Sum. Theol.,* III, 12, 2; cf. above, Section 3) was not yet the case in his *Commentary on the Sentences,* —the existence in Jesus of an experimental science acquired through the power of the agent intellect, in conformity with the mode of thinking essential to the nature of the *animal rationale,* and of the *verus homo.* Unlike that which he holds to be true on the subject of the grace of Christ and of His infused science, St. Thomas recognizes even, let us note carefully, that the *habitus* itself of this acquired experimental science *has progressively increased in Jesus: Secundum hanc scientiam, Christus non a principio scivit omnia: sed paulatim et post aliquod tempus: scilicet in perfecta aetate; quod patet ex hoc quod Evangelista simul dicit eum profecisse scientia et aetate (ibid.,* ad 1). —And the Gospel does not say this only of the science of Christ, it says it also of His grace, I permit myself to observe.

But on other points concerning the presence in Jesus of this acquired experimental science, let us dare to say that St. Thomas had not yet completely freed himself of the ancient views. To admit that through such an acquired experimental science, Jesus (once come to the plenitude of age) knew *all that which is knowable by the light of the agent intellect* (III,

117

which He knew of His divinity and of His mission through His infused science.

25. I have already noted that the knowledge through infused science that Jesus had of His own divinity developed during the childhood of Jesus probably very quickly. This is to say that the *consciousness that Jesus had of His own divinity* also developed very quickly in the course of His childhood.

And if this was so, it is not only owing to the natural intuitivity proper to the child, it is also for a more profound reason, because it is entirely unthinkable that the fact of *being God* should have one day irrupted into the consciousness of an adolescent who up to that moment would have had consciousness of Himself without being yet informed of such a fact, while on the other hand the idea of God would have already taken form in Him. He would have been simply crushed by such a revelation (before which, besides, He would have taken himself for a mere man,

---

12, 1c and ad 3), —and therefore, for example, (and still better than they) all that which our learned men know, and their successors will know, of topology, of atomic physics, of biology, of ethnology, etc.; to admit also that He *learned nothing from men* (III, 12, 3), because *it was not fitting to his dignity that He be taught by any man,* seems to me incompatible with the *secundum modum connaturalem homini* that it is necessary to recognize for the very acquisition of the experimental science, and for the comportment of the *verus homo* insofar precisely as viator. Does not this acquisition essentially imply the inevitable limitations due to the historical succession of cultures and to the short duration of a man's life? And did not the Child Jesus learn from His Mother, just as all children here on earth, His *maternal tongue?* And how would the fact of learning anything at all from a man have detracted from the dignity of He who came in perfect humility and to the dignity of whom it was not contrary to walk as a poor man on the roads, and to be treated as a blasphemer by the Doctors of the Law, and scourged, covered with spittle, crowned with thorns, derided by Herod, condemned to death by a despicable Roman procurator, put on the Cross like the worst criminals?

and, —another impossibility in that which concerns Christ, — would have to that extent been in error).

It is, therefore, absolutely necessary that the consciousness of His own divinity should have surged up in Jesus from the instant that He began to become conscious of Himself, and that there began to germinate the idea of God in His acquired science as in His infused science at the state of way; it is absolutely necessary also that it should have grown progressively at the same time as developed His consciousness of Himself, and that the idea of God took better and better shape in His mind, thanks to the infused *species* meeting and illuminating from above the notions communicated from here below through the blessed voice of His Mother and the sacred rites of the Law. The wonder connatural to childhood gave way to the supernatural wonder of the revelation of Himself to Himself. It is without the least surprise, and in a manner altogether harmonious, fresh and gracious, it is with all the naturalness, and the admirable simplicity, and the admirable seriousness of the little child regarding being [74] that the Child Jesus knew that He was God, and that this consciousness of His divinity underwent in Him its developments.

I think that it had been preceded by a light of infused science at its first dawn, given to the little Child the moment He opened His eyes, —long before any knowledge reflectively conscious, — and which, later, as soon as the intelligence in Him had performed its first-initial-act (as soon as it had itself opened its eyes), had illuminated His dawning consciousness of Himself, —of Himself and of His divinity.

Then came the progressive development of which I have just

74. *L'être étonne dans les yeux de l'enfant*
    Et refuse de voir le monde.
(Raïssa Maritain, *L'Échelle,* in Poèmes inédits, *Nova et Vetera,* 1963, III.)

spoken. And this consciousness of His divinity did not have to delay very much to become perfect or complete, —which does not mean that once complete it did not continue to grow, just as the grace itself, and the wisdom itself, and the charity itself, had continued to grow until the instant that Jesus gave up His soul into the hands of the Father.

What seems clear to me, in any case, is that it had already attained its point of perfect maturity [75] at the time when He remained in the Temple, unbeknown to Mary and Joseph, in order to hear and question the Doctors. He was twelve years old then; and He was in full possession, even conceptual, of His knowledge of the things of God, and of His consciousness of Himself as God. *A Patre exivi; antequam Abraham fierat, ego sum:* from that moment He would have been able to say this to them. It was the first time that the Son of God faced the world of the Doctors and of the scribes. He had *to be about His Father's business;* He, this Child who knew Himself *Primogenitus a Patre,* who knew Himself the Word Incarnate, and Incarnate for the work of the Redemption to be accomplished, He was going to see that which these people thought of divine things and of the accomplishment of the prophecies. He was to return from it quite grieved.

THEANDRIC ACTION

26. Permit me to propose further some remarks on that which Pseudo-Dionysius, followed by the theological tradition, calls

75. The consciousness that Jesus had of His divinity was to be much higher still at the time of the Last Supper and of the appearance before Caiphas. What I mean is that at twelve years of age, before the Doctors, He had already, with the full consciousness of His divinity, a science of the divine things more perfect and more ample than that of any man here on earth.

theandric action or *theandric operation,* which was characteristic of Christ.

I have recalled already [76] that each time that one designates Christ, it is His Person which one designates, that is the divine Word, and that it is therefore permissible to say: "Christ has made the heavens and the earth," —or again, as St. Jude according to the Vulgate,[77] that "Jesus saved His people from the land of Egypt," and has kept in everlasting chains "the angels also who did not preserve their original state, but forsook their abode." [78]

When one expresses himself thus, he speaks of actions or operations which the Word, Person of Jesus, has accomplished as God and without using the human nature hypostatically assumed. These are not theandric operations.

That which Dionysius calls a theandric action or operation, it is an operation *one* in that which concerns the subject from which it proceeds, but *double* by reason of the two natures of the latter,[79] —so that one has there a *divine* operation and a *human* operation, the first making use instrumentally of the second.

Well, it seems to me that being granted the theandric character of all the actions or operations of Jesus during His earthly life, there is reason to distinguish in them two different kinds of categories.

For an agent can move a thing either in proposing to himself simply to bring into play that which is proper to it, or with a view to producing thanks to it an effect which by itself alone it is incapable of reaching. I can move my legs simply in order to give them exercise while I walk, or I can move my arms and my hands

76. Cf. above, Section 3.
77. Jude, 5-6.
78. "Admirable faith in Jesus present and acting in His divine preexistence," Raïssa wrote (*Journal de Raïssa,* p. 298).
79. Cf. *Sum. Theol.,* III, 19, 1c and ad 3.

with a view to making a work of art. In the two cases, I use my members instrumentally; but in the first case it is only through a certain *mode* proper to my walking that there appears in the action accomplished a reflection of my personality; in the second case, it is through the *work* produced itself. Another example: I can move a vase of flowers in order to change its place on the table, or I can ply a saw and a plane in order to make, supposing that I am competent in this art, a piece of cabinet-work. In the two cases I use instrumentally the objects in question; but in the first case the quality of my mental operation shows itself only in the *manner,* pleasing or displeasing to the eye, in which the flowers set off to advantage their own appearances in the spot where I have placed them; in the second case, it is in a *work* produced that reveals itself my virtue of principal agent passing through the tools which I use.

I ask, therefore: Was it not the same for the actions which the Lord accomplished here on earth, and which were all theandric operations?

When He raised the dead, the divine operation passed through the human operation, —through the human words of Jesus: *Lazare, veni foras!* —in order to produce a *work* of which no purely human operation is capable.

When He ate and drank in the home of Levi, the son of Alpheus, or walked on the roads with His disciples, or "went," unharmed, among the men who hated Him, the divine operation only passed through the operation of the human faculties in order to impress a certain *mode* on that which the latter did according to their own virtue.[80]

The manner of Jesus! The style of Jesus! Fortunate were those

80. I have glossed freely the *ambulatio* and the *sanatio* of the ad 3 of III, 19, 1.

who were able to know them with their own eyes! The thousand actions which He did like everyone else, He did them as no one else, —in a manner unique in the world. *Transiens per medium illorum, ibat.* He went about, passing into the midst of them, — yes, with what simple majesty, with what peace, what tranquil and gentle assurance, which prevented any hand from setting itself upon Him!

27. My second remark, on the subject of theandric operations, concerns those in which it is in order to produce some suprahuman work that the human operation was instrumentally superelevated by the divine operation.

The human operation was *divinely* superelevated, certainly, since it was superelevated by the very operation of the divine Word. In order to know this, however, it was necessary to know who Jesus was.

For anyone who saw such works from without, they gave evidence, no doubt, of a supernatural power; one knew (if one was of good faith) that they could come only from a blessed one of God. None, however, even the raising of Lazarus, could be a proof of the divinity of Jesus. Did He not, moreover, promise His disciples that, under the motion of His grace, they would do—they, simple men—works greater still than His own? *Qui credit in me, opera, quae ego facio, et ipse faciet, et majora horum faciet.*[81]

Let us say summarily that that which the works, the signs (and the preaching, and the whole personal comportment, and the mercy, and the goodness . . .) proved is the *holiness* of Christ and His divine mission. And it was clear that such a holy one, such a man sent from God, such a beloved of God could not de-

81. Jn. 14, 12.

ceive. So that it is His own words, His own testimony concerning Himself, which were to be for men the irrecusable proof of His *divinity*.

In reflecting upon this, one is better able to see certain things.

If Jesus has so often and in so many ways, constantly as it were, alluded to His divinity, but in keeping during so long a time such discretion, such silence, with regard to that which concerns the explicit affirmation of it, is it not that that which the wisdom of the Father wanted is that first the holiness and the mission of the Son should be rendered evident to men? Time was required for this. There was required three years of preaching of the Kingdom, and of labor, and of miracles, in order for this holiness and this mission to be firmly recognized by the disciples, and more or less weakly discerned by many in the crowd. And after that, when the last hour had come, it is before Caiphas that Jesus was to affirm finally, in an explicit, clear, and decisive manner, that He was the Son of God. And Caiphas understood well that which was said to him, but blind to the holiness of Jesus he tore his garments and cried, "He has blasphemed!" That is how the divinity of Jesus was to be for the first time publicly proclaimed by Him.

Previously, it is to the small circle of disciples that it had been confided, and as discreetly as possible. How instructive is the Gospel in this respect! To reply publicly to the question which everybody was asking himself: *Who is this man?* would have served only to satisfy a shallow curiosity. One day when His little flock was gathered, Jesus still had refrained from making a declaration on this subject; He had questioned His disciples. "Who do men say the Son of Man is? . . . But who do you say that I am?" And it is Peter who had answered: "Thou art the Christ, the son of the living God." And Jesus had only confirmed the words of Peter: "Blessed art thou, Simon Barjona, for flesh and blood has not revealed this to thee, but my Father in heaven." [82] That which was of essential, eternal, importance was not a declaration outwardly proferred, be it by Jesus Himself; it was the revelation made by the Father to the heart of Peter, son of Jona. The faith of Peter, the revelation received by Him from the Father, forever, and the assistance and the inspiration assured him, —behold the rock, on which Christ would build His Church.

And then, how does the recital of Peter's avowal end? After His solemn promises to Peter, what does Jesus do? "He strictly charged his disciples to tell no one that he was Jesus the Christ . . ." [83]

*　　*　　*

The Kingdom of God is a handful of leaven in the world. " 'To what shall I liken the kingdom of God? It is like leaven, which a woman took and buried in three measures of flour, until all of it was leavened'." [84] Then she puts the dough in the oven, and she has bread.

Take pounds of flour in order to make a great mass of dough. And knead this dough, prepare it, *organize it* in the most beautiful manner, but without leaven, or with flat leaven. And put it in the oven, —it will be good only for the flies.

The Christians who think that the Kingdom of God comes in noise and din, and who would like to cause to pass to the front rank of its equipment the resources of modern publicity and of the *mass media of communication* (without suspecting that all these means tend by nature to serve the illusory more than the true) would no doubt do well to reread a little the Gospel.

82. Matt. 16, 13-17.
83. Matt. 16, 20.
84. Lk. 13, 20-21.

IV. From Adolescence to the Death on the Cross

28. On the third stage of the life of Christ, —the hidden life in Nazareth, —I would like to note briefly two things.

First of all, it was a period of incomparable contemplative life, superior to all that which one can conceive. Jesus was from that time onwards at the most elevated state of the mystical life, and it is in this most elevated state that the mystical life grew in Him until the end. I have said that there was a translucid partition between the supraconscious paradise of the soul of Christ and the world of the consciousness or of the here-below of this soul: this means that from the supraconscious nothing could *descend* in order to specify the conscious activities; [1] it is only general comfortings and a participated light, in particular the light communicated to the infused science, which descended into the world of consciousness.

But with regard to the inverse movement, the movement of *ascent* or of *ascension,* the translucid partition was penetrable. As I said at the beginning (Section 6), through His infused contemplation Jesus entered, in order to take there His repose and

---

1. There was one moment when in the soul of Christ the kind of partition of which I am speaking was taken away by miracle, —when the Vision and the divinization which proceeds from it invaded and transformed the entire soul, and the body itself of Jesus, —when the state of viator was eclipsed by the state of comprehensor; it is the moment of the Transfiguration, anticipation of glory.

His joy, into the supraconscious paradise of His soul, where enraptured in union with God His consciousness of viator approached almost His Vision as comprehensor,[2] and where He experienced the divine things according to that savory experience of love which the gifts of the Holy Spirit give, and which in Christ-viator was incomparably higher than in any other man, quite near, and more and more near, without however attaining it, the point of unsurpassable perfection (asymptotic) proper to Christ-comprehensor.

In the second place, it seems to me that it is reasonable to think that from the moment when He was found among the Doctors, and especially once an adult, Jesus revealed progressively to Joseph and to Mary *absolutely all the mysteries of God* which He had come in order to announce. In view of their immense mutual love, how would He have been able not to communicate to them, to

2. The Beatific Vision itself remained clearly proper to Jesus as comprehensor. It is as comprehensor, —but I believe, never as viator, even in the most elevated states of contemplative union, —that Christ had on earth the Vision of the divine essence. I know well that St. Thomas, though teaching in the most categorical manner that no man-viator can see God through His essence (I, 12, 11), made exception for St. Paul and for Moses (II-II, 175, 3), in his desire to follow the opinions of St. Augustine wherever he found the least possibility to do so. Nevertheless, how would St. Augustine have been able to know what took place in St. Paul better than St. Paul himself, who assures us of the *words* which he has heard, but not at all of that which he would have *seen,* when he was "caught up into Paradise"? *"Et scio hujusmodi hominem sive in corpore sive extra corpus nescio, Deus scit, quoniam raptus est in paradisum et audivit arcana verba quae non licet hominem loqui"* (2 Cor. 12, 3-4). It seems certainly preferable to adhere strictly to the *non videbit me homo* [*homo viator*] *et vivet* of Exodus (33, 20), and to the demonstration of St. Thomas in the body of the article to which I refer in the first lines of this note (I, 12, 11). There is no common measure between the rapture of St. Paul and the Beatific Vision of Christ, —nor between the sense that it is necessary to give to the word *"audivit"* used by Jesus in Jn. 8, 26 (cf. above, p. 105) and that which it is necessary to give to the *"audivit arcana verba"* of St. Paul.

128

them first, that which He was to communicate to the apostles and to all men?

No doubt Mary in a sense already knew all this, —I mean that in the supraconscious of her soul (not divinized by the Vision like that of Jesus, and simply human like that of each of us, and suffused with grace), the illumination produced by the words of the angel at the moment of the Annunciation, —"Behold, thou shalt conceive in thy womb and shalt bring forth a son; and thou shalt call his name Jesus. He shall be great, and shall be called the Son of the Most High; and the Lord God will give him the throne of David his father, and he shall be king over the house of Jacob forever; and of his kingdom there shall be no end . . ."[3] "The Holy Spirit shall come upon thee and the power of the Most High shall overshadow thee,"[4] —caused her to know in a flash all the mysteries of salvation, and above all the fact that the Child conceived by her was God Incarnate. But all this knowledge remained supraconscious: only diffuse rays of it passed into her consciousness; that which she knew consciously that day, and was able to say to herself in concepts was only that through a miracle of the Almighty she would give birth to the Saviour of Israel, whose reign would last without end, He whose arrival here on earth would invert all human values, would depose the powerful and would exalt the humble. Is it not this that appears to us from an attentive reading of the *Magnificat?* [5] Is this not why she

3. Lk. 1, 32-33.
4. *Ibid.,* 35.
5. Why should it be astonishing that the *Magnificat* resembles the canticle of Anna (1 Sam. 2, 1-10)? The soul of Mary was entirely nourished on holy Scripture.
When one writes, as certain people do today, that the canticle of Anna served as "model" for the Magnificat of Luke, one no doubt renders homage to the transcendent and well-assured superiority which erudition does not ask better than to recognize for itself with regard to whatever

129

was so eager to *keep in her heart* all that which on the side of men (of the shepherds at Bethlehem, of the old man Simeon, of the prophetess Anna) was said of the mystery of her Son? Is this not why she and Joseph, when they, after having been very anxious, found the Child Jesus in the Temple, *did not understand*[6] His answer: "How is it that you sought me? Did you not know that I must be about my Father's business?"

One can think, as I indicated a few moments ago, that this conversation with the Doctors of the Temple has marked the beginning of the communications through which, once returned to Nazareth, Jesus began to confide to these two loved ones—by

---

objects are submitted to it. But one forgets for a moment that, in order to express that which was deepest in their soul, the saints of Israel were accustomed to bring into play the themes, nay the words themselves, already consecrated by the divine wisdom and by its prophets. The canticle of Anna has served as "source of lyrical expression" for the Magnificat of Mary. Moreover, Anna, who rendered thanks to God for no longer being sterile, did not say in her canticle that *all generations would call her blessed.*

6. *Non intellexerunt verbum, quod locutus est ad eos* (Lk. 2, 50). —If Joseph and Mary did not understand that which Jesus replied to them at that time, is it not that they had raised Him as every other child is raised in the midst of his family, and that, taking care not to tell Him anything of His miraculous conception, they had, *they thought,* let Him believe that Joseph was His father (*"Fili, quid fecisti nobis sic? Ecce pater tuus et ego dolentes quaerebamus te"*), according to the ordinary idea which in every family the child forms quite frankly of his father, without his knowing anything yet of that which generation is? I think it is once back at Nazareth, after the conversation with the Doctors, that the Child Jesus who, up till then had played the game in keeping silent began quite gently to exercise His mission of true and supreme Doctor, leading first of all Mary and Joseph to understand that He knew (through His infused science) the mystery of His procreation here on earth through the virtue of the Most High, and telling them also that of His eternal procreation by the Father, —in short, beginning, as I indicate here, to teach them progressively, under mode of communicable concepts, all the mysteries of revelation (which in another manner, as I indicate also, they knew already, but inexpressibly).

what a sublime and gentle initiation in which He spoke from the abundance of the heart, without need of figures and of parables— the secrets of the uncreated Life and those of the Redemption. Then Mary *recognized,* in a contemplation filled with wonder (conscious participation, now that Jesus taught her and in proportion as He taught her, of the prophetic illumination received at the Annunciation), that which she *knew* already in the heights of the supraconscious, but which remained there hidden to her conscious thought: admirable teaching, which, in lifting progressively the veils of the holy Truth with which her mind was already filled, revealed to her at once the Inaccessible and the sacred treasures already present in her.

And that which I have just said of Mary, it is fitting to hold as likewise true, though on a less elevated plane, of St. Joseph, whose incomparably profound faith recognized also, in the words of Jesus, unformulated truths virtually contained in the mystery of full theological adhesion.

I understand well that the life of the Holy Family was, above all, a life of recollection, and of adoring silence.[7] But it is not conceivable that the Word remained silent during so many years in the presence of ears so holy and so dear and so perfectly attentive. A few words were enough for Him in order to throw into abysses of light the two who listened to Him. And why would they have

7. Father Surin, in the letter in which he tells of his trip with "the young man of the coach," —and in which, as Julian Green suggests in his beautiful preface to the *Correspondance* edited by Father de Certeau, he lent doubtless many of the thoughts which in reality were his own to this strange companion, —assures us that "St. Joseph had been a man of great silence; that in the house of our Lord he spoke very little, but our Lady still less and our Lord even less than either of them." This is true no doubt, although the saintly Jesuit whom I venerate was naturally inclined to some excess. But just the same the Word was there, and however little He spoke He said much.

deprived themselves of questioning their God who was living with them His human life.

29. Thus at Nazareth, Jesus, while leading a life of manual work and of mystical contemplation that was all that which there is of the most sublime, was the *Illuminator* and the *Sanctifier* of Mary and of Joseph. It is they who first received the Gospel, and with an unsurpassable plenitude. Then the Holy Family, during all the hidden life, appears as the Church of the New Law, wholly concentrated in three persons.

It is this which we were saying in our first meeting, and which causes us to conceive the Holy Family as something infinitely more elevated than a simple model of the domestic virtues. It was a Church *sine macula, sine ruga,* not only in its essential life but in the individual behavior of its members,[8] however unequal were their degrees of perfection and of holiness, —the one being the Word Incarnate Himself, comprehensor and viator at one and the same time, come in order to accomplish through His sacrifice the work of the Redemption of the human race, and whose grace was the capital grace on which the Church lives; [9] the other being

---

Surin writes further, and here I believe him more willingly: "He added to me that he had known clearly from this holy patriarch that he was the greatest of saints after the Virgin; that he had the fullness of the Holy Spirit quite otherwise than the apostles; that he was ruler over the souls whose virtue must be hidden in this world, just as his had been; that he was so little known; that in recompense God willed that it should be only souls extremely pure who would have lights touching his grandeurs." *Correspondance de Jean-Joseph Surin,* Paris, 1966, p. 142.

8. In this sense, it was, as it were, a prefiguration of the Church of Heaven.

9. *"De plenitudine ejus nos omnes accepimus"* (Jn. 1, 16). Cf. *Sum. Theol.,* III, 8, 5: "The personal grace whereby the soul of Christ is justified is essentially the same as His grace according as He is head of the Church justifying others; but it differs according to 'ratio'."

the *Theotokos,* Immaculate from her conception, sheer creature but which touches the confines of divinity; the third not having this unique privilege but being the first and the greatest Saint of the New Law among those who share the human condition.

This Church of the New Law has taken shape in the womb of the Old Law, in the manner of a germ, in a secret and hidden fashion, somewhat like before being born outwardly a child takes shape in the womb of its mother. There was then a regime of the *New Law* which began, and at first for three persons only, while the regime of the *Old Law* continued for all the other Jews.

It is when Jesus enters into the fourth stage of His life, the period of the public life, and when He preaches and teaches and

---

It is, therefore, from the creation of the soul of Jesus that His grace (this grace which in the paradise of His soul was infinite in its order, and which in the here-below of His soul was higher than that of any man but finite in its order and increased with the years) was capital grace. In our view, it is by reason of two different modes that it is necessary to conceive how, from the very moment that Christ had come, all those who received the grace received it from His plenitude.

On one hand (first mode), during the intra-uterine life of Christ and His early childhood (and later, even at the time of His public life, with regard to the men who were not a part of the little flock of His disciples, or were not of those on whom, among the multitudes who had the good fortune to see Him, a special glance of His love was directed), it is of the grace of Christ *as habitus* (without intervention of the will of Jesus Himself) that God made use instrumentally in order to sanctify souls.

On the other hand (second mode), from the moment that Jesus was able to put in play His infused science in a conceptual and discursive manner and through initiatives of His free will, —and therefore from His adolesence and from the life of Nazareth (with regard to Mary and Joseph), then, during His public life (with regard to the apostles, the disciples, the holy women, the Samaritan woman, etc.), —it is by reason of the *wisdom and of the mercy in act and of the voluntary decisions of Christ himself* that His grace flowed onto souls in order to sanctify them.

Finally, it is only after the Resurrection, and in the glorious Christ to whom the Father has restored the Kingdom, that this second mode of operation of capital grace extended itself to the universality of men.

133

illumines, that the Church of the New Law or of Christ *come* begins to spread itself among men,[10] —the apostles, the disciples, the holy women, and also all those whom He causes to be reborn through His grace and to whom He says: "Thy sins are forgiven thee, go and sin no more."

But this Church of the New Law continues still to develop in the womb of the regime of the Old Law, and so to speak masked by it. The regime of the Old Law is crumbling, it is not yet abolished. It will be abolished only on the day of the Crucifixion, when the veil of the Temple is rent. And it is only at Pentecost that the umbilical cord, if I may say, will be broken. And there will be required still a certain time for one to become aware of it, —there will be required a vision sent to St. Peter, and, above all, the preaching of St. Paul.

To return to the period of the public life of Jesus: I will not discuss the forty days of fasting and of the three temptations which were the preface to it; I will note only that this period has been clearly that of the supreme growths of the infused science of Christ, as of His gift of prophecy, and of His other charisms such as the gift of miracles.

THE AGONY IN THE GARDEN, AND THE CROSS

30. Of the fifth stage,[11] Agony and Passion, I have already said a few words previously. At that time Jesus in His prayer could no longer penetrate with His consciousness into the supraconscious

10. In this case it is not of a *prefiguration* of the Church of Heaven, it is of the *establishment* of the militant Church that it is necessary to think.

11. I recall that in order to show the intimate link between the Crucifixion and the Resurrection, I have designated the Agony and the Cross as stage 5, and the Resurrection as stage 5a.

paradise of His soul; all experience, through His conscious faculties, of this paradise and of its radiance was refused to Him, it was the night of the spirit at its absolutely supreme degree, —at the moment of the Agony as at that of the fourth Word on the Cross: *Ut quid dereliquisti me?*

And during the Agony in the garden and the sweating of blood, His human will desired ardently, —I do not say willed by an act of free decision, an act of choice, God forbid! —I say: *desired,* with all the weight of its nature, something other than that which the will of God willed. And the chalice whose removal He asked, if it was possible, was not only the cruel death and the torments of the Passion and the horror of the sacrifice, it was also all the evil of the human race, evil of sin or of offense of God and evil of suffering, all that evil which He saw gathered together and which He was to assume, yes, in order to redeem us, but which was to continue until the end of time and of which with the most profound élan of His desires of nature, He *did not want* the existence, whether it is a question of the evil of suffering just as of the evil of sin. For it seems to me (it is a hypothesis which I submit to you), that in its *desires of nature* the human will of Jesus was consonant with the antecedent will of God, which wills the salvation of every man, and also his happiness. Be that as it may, during the Agony in the garden, this human will, which according to all the power of its attractions and desires *of nature* was other than that of the Father, was, through its *free* disposition of itself, *entirely and perfectly submitted* to the will of the Father, to the *consequent* will of God. Let *Thy* will be done, and *not mine.* It was obedience at its supreme degree of perfection.

And when one finally reaches the death on the Cross, then I would like to insist a little on the moment, —it seems to me that this constitutes but one moment, a last time, a single *ultimum tempus,* —of the sixth Word: *It is consummated,* and of the seventh Word: *Father, into thy hands I commend my spirit.* Then Christ does not will only that the will of His Father and not His be done; it is, in love at its supreme conceivable degree, in love which consummates and transcends obedience, His own will, absolutely one with that of the Father, which He accomplishes, in an act of supreme sacrifice and of supreme freedom.[12]

Come to this point, what can we think of the mysterious remark which one reads in Jn. 10, 18: *"No one takes it [my life; my soul] from me, but I lay it down of myself. I have the power to lay it down, and I have the power to take it up again"?* St. Thomas, as far as I know, does not enlighten us very much on this point. In Part II, q. 50, a. 1, ad 2, he says that Christ "has undergone a death coming from without, to which He spontaneously offered Himself, in order that His death *appear indeed as voluntary"* and not as due "to the necessity of dying as a result of the infirmity of nature," which refers to another question. And when he comes in the *Summa* [13] to the remark related by St. John, he contents himself (q. 50, a. 3, ad 1) with repeating St. Augustine

---

12. It is at this supreme moment of the life of Christ-*viator* that His merit becomes *infinite,* —merit for the perfect reparation of the offense made to the Father by all the sins of the world, merit for the universality of the human race, for the salvation of all men; and merit also for Himself, with regard to His own entry into glory and into the universal lordship at the right hand of the Father. (And also with regard to that Beatific Vision itself which in virtue of the hypostatic union He had received as a gift from the creation of His soul, but of which it belonged to Him moreover to render Himself worthy through His merits as man, attesting in this even His condition of *verus homo.*)

13. With the Commentary on St. John (cap. 10, lect. 4), the mind is not more satisfied. That which one presents to it is a sort of metaphysical suicide accomplished by the will of a *non purus homo* conceived in a manner which we can only regard as incompatible with the *verus homo.*

when the latter declares that it is not the Word who has laid down His soul (in which case the soul at the moment of the death of Christ would have been separated from the Word, which is false); and it is not the soul which has been separated from itself, which is absurd; it remains, therefore, that it is the *flesh,* it is the flesh which has *laid down its soul,* and which afterwards has taken it up again, not by its own power, but by the power of the Word inhabiting the flesh. This is an explanation which truly leaves little room for the free human will of Christ, which seems clearly affirmed in St. John.

Well, is it that in the view which I am proposing another explanation is not possible?

In this view, the moment in question, the moment of the sixth and of the seventh Words, the *ultimum tempus* of the earthly life of Christ, is precisely the point where the ascending oblique straight line of which I spoke at the beginning, and which symbolizes the constant growth in grace and in charity all through the earthly life of Christ as *viator, meets* the horizontal straight line which symbolizes the supreme and unsurpassable perfection, —excluding all possibility of growth, —of this same grace and of this same charity of Christ as *comprehensor,* according as during His earthly life they reigned infinite in the supraconscious

---

"*In Christo autem natura sua et tota alia natura subditur voluntati ejus, sicut artificiata voluntati artificis.*" This is true only of the divine will of the Word *as not using* human nature. Moreover, in the *Summa Theologica,* St. Thomas teaches that the soul of Christ did not have omnipotence with regard to the mutation of creatures (III, 13, 2) nor with regard to His own body (III, 13, 3); and later, in q. 47, a. 1, where he rejects decidedly every idea of that which I have just called a sort of metaphysical suicide, he diminishes singularly the import of the remark reported by St. John: "*Cum dicitur: nemo tollit animam meam, intelligitur: me invito.*"

paradise of His soul, and as afterwards they continue to reign infinite in the glorious Christ during eternity.

What is it that takes place in fact at the moment of which I am speaking?

Christ, the Word divine acting through the instrumentality of His human will, *wills* the sacrifice, wills to give to the very end His life (human) for His friends, wills to *lay down this life,* wills to *die* in order to satisfy in justice all the sins of the human race and in order to redeem all men. In other words, He wills that there be *separated the one from the other,* by the most total and terrible rupture which human nature can undergo, that flesh and that soul whose substantial union constitutes His own life, the human life which He has assumed.

And this holocaust Christ wills *through love,* through love for His Father and through love for men. There is no greater love. At this moment the charity of Christ who is still viator crosses the abyss which separates the finite from the infinite, it is brought to the degree of perfection supreme and unsurpassable (asymptotic) where exists the charity of Christ as comprehensor, it *becomes infinite in its order;* it is love at the highest degree conceivable in a created nature, —beyond the whole infinite series of the possible degrees of increasing perfection, —at the summit of the mystical union where, according to the remark of St. John of the Cross, man and God are "a single spirit and love," —but this time in an ecstasy of the soul in God so total and so powerful that human nature cannot endure it and it tears the soul from the body.

In other words, it is through an ecstasy of love that Christ has died on the Cross, at the height of the freedom of the will, and delivered His soul into the hands of the Father.

This supreme love of Christ-viator come to the degree of union with God proper to Christ-comprehensor has been the love from which Christ-viator died, because such an act of love is incompatible with the joining of the soul with the flesh and with its finitude. It is, if I may say, the "let go!" of the soul. It is this which caused Christ to die, it is this way that His will of sacrifice has been accomplished, and that He has, —He, the Word divine acting through the instrumentality of His human will, —freely "laid down His soul," in separating it, not from the Word itself, indeed, but *from its flesh,* in other words, from the human life of the Word Incarnate.

Here it is necessary to recall this fundamental truth that in every action and passion it is always the *supposit* or the *person* which acts or which suffers; and it is necessary to remember that this truth imposes imperiously its law on our language. It is the Person of the Word which did and suffered all that Christ did and suffered—through the instrumentality of His human nature.

Is it, therefore, necessary for us to say that just as Mary, because she is the Mother of Christ, is the *Mother of God,* so also the death of Christ has been the *death of God?* Yes, it is necessary to say this, although it runs the risk of being terribly misunderstood. This did not impede Hegel from saying it, when he wished to translate into his forger's dialectic that which took place on Good Friday.

And after Hegel, Nietzsche was again to take up this word in a sense which, instead of pretending itself still Christian, blasphemed Christianity in order to announce purely and simply the death of God, replaced by the superman.

It remains nevertheless true, provided that one understands correctly that which one says, that on Good Friday *a divine Person died* (a human death), the Word Incarnate died, died of love and voluntarily. It is a very shocking expression, but if one refuses shocking expressions, one renounces glimpsing however little the mystery of the Cross. *Unus de Trinitate mortuus est,* one of the members of the Trinity has died, it is the formula which the Second Council of Constantinople has employed. Here is the scandal of the Cross.

And at the Resurrection, it is this same *Unus de Trinitate,* it is the Word Incarnate who takes up again His human life. It is He, it is this same divine Person, —who had been the *Person of Christ* as long as Christ was living, —who communicates *to His human soul* (which remained hypostatically united to Him) the power of uniting itself again, through an act of His free will, to its body (which had remained hypostatically united to the Word).

In other words, the Word uses instrumentally His human soul in order to *take up again* this same soul as substantially *united to the Body;* the Word has triumphed over death through the means of His humanity.

31. If it is permissible to cast one's eyes on a thing as sacred, infinitely terrible, and infinitely holy as the death of the Word Incarnate, I would like still, in order to conclude this study, to add a few words.

I have said that Jesus died of a supreme ecstasy of love in which His charity of *viator* (proper to the here-below of His soul) rejoined the infinity of His charity of *comprehensor* (proper to the heaven of His soul). He had suffered the Agony in the garden. There was no agony on the Cross,[14] but only the suffering, and, at the end, death, at once inflicted through violence and voluntary.

Attention here! The nails and the tearing asunder on the Cross

14. The *Deus, Deus meus, quare dereliquisti me* is not a cry of agony, wrested by the struggle against the death which is approaching. It is the last lamentation of the soul in Him from whom, because of the sin assumed by Him, God Himself seems to withdraw, in order to exhaust on Him His justice: the whole affair being here between Christ and God.

led of themselves to the death, this is true; the violence inflicted was death on the way: but it was only this. It is not the violence inflicted which finally caused the separation of the soul and of the body: Jesus died sooner than the executioners expected, whereas the two thieves lived yet (and they would have lived still longer if one had not broken their legs); why this unusually quick death, unless because that which has caused the separation of the soul and of the body, that which has really *caused to die* Jesus, it is, —in advance of the death which the inflicted violence would have produced, —His supreme act of love offering His *all,* His very being of man, for the salvation of the world and the accomplishment of the designs of the Father.

St. Thomas remarks [15] that death can be considered in two ways: either *secundum quod est in fieri,* according as it *is going to be,* —"when someone tends towards death through some passion either natural or violent," —or *secundum quod est in facto esse,* according as it is accomplished, and "as has already taken place the separation of the soul and of the body."

We must apply this distinction also to the death of Jesus through ecstasy of love.

If we consider the death of Jesus *secundum quod est in facto esse,* it is necessary to say that at the instant at which His supreme act of love *had caused His death,* at the instant at which He *was dead,* then His soul, entered into glory and eternity, and being henceforth under the state only of *comprehensor,* finds itself already, even before the Resurrection, prepared to exercise (after the Ascension, once the Man resurrected is "seated at the right hand of the Father"), the universal government which will never cease, and through which He applies the merits of His Passion and of His Death to all the men who will not refuse His grace.

15. *Sum. Theol.,* III, 50, 6.

(It is only as Uncreated Word that Christ made the application of the "foreseen" redemptive merit to the men who lived before Him on the earth, saved if their freedom did not stand in the way of grace.)

But if we consider the death of Christ *secundum quod est in fieri,* it is necessary to say that at the end, in the moment, however brief it may be, at which He *is going to die,* at which His soul *is going to* leave His body, He lives still, and with what supreme intensity: it is the moment at which He *delivers* His soul into the hands of the Father, and at which His charity of viator *rejoins* the infinity of His charity of comprehensor, and *will cause* thus the separation of the soul and of the body. At this moment one must think, according to the hypothesis which I propose, that, at the same stroke, His infused science, such as in the here-below of His soul it found itself under the state of way, *makes room* for His infused science such as in the heaven of His soul it found itself already under the state of term or of consummation, where it will remain always: at this brief moment, therefore, in the moment that He *is going to die,* Jesus, while His love more living than ever breaks the bonds which still hold back His soul, enters with all His psychic life and His consciousness still in the state of way into the heaven of His soul, and there, through His Beatific Vision and through His infinite infused science, knows no longer only in a supraconscious manner, but in His very consciousness of expiring viator, each human being singularly taken together with his secret thoughts, *omnia existentia secundum quodcumque tempus,* in short, *each* of those for whom He gives His life; and through His charity of viator joining, at this brief moment, the infinity of His charity of comprehensor, He loves then each one *in his singular reality,* He loves him as if he was alone in the world. According to the saying of Pascal, which it is necessary to take up again here in modifying it a little, Jesus says to each one of us: On my Cross, at the last moment, I gave my life *for you,* I loved you to the point of dying for you.

Finally, supposing (as I hope) that these reflections are exact, it is fitting to push them yet a little further. If, by reason of the atrocious cruelty of the Cross, by reason also of the supremely delicate sensibility of His body, received from the immaculate Virgin, the Death of Christ considered *in fieri,* —His passage, from the crowning with thorns and the carrying of the Cross up until the ninth hour, through the gates which at the last moment open onto the rupture of terrestrial existence, —has been a death unimaginably painful, what must one say, nevertheless, of the last moment of this *fieri,* at which, just before the end, His consciousness of viator has opened onto the infinite infused science and the Vision of the divine essence and the supreme, infinite charity shut up till then in the supraconscious heaven of His soul? It was the Beatific Vision and the Beatific Love at their sovereign degree; and, consequently, has not this final moment been a blessed moment? Yes, it is necessary to say that after nameless sufferings the final moment at which Jesus has delivered His soul into the hands of the Father has been a Death infinitely blessed: Death of Victim more than ever, but of Victim entering already into the beatitude which the instant of Death *in facto esse* was to seal for eternity.

And is it not necessary to say also that at an infinite distance from this Death of the Son of God, but nevertheless in a certain analogy with it, those among us who die in the Lord, be it sometimes after a frightful agony, and sometimes also without agony, open, at the final moment of their life here on earth, just before the entry into death, onto that eternal life which has been merited for them by their Redeemer, and which, from the instant that they will have entered into death, is going to continue for them into the centuries of centuries? It is not uncommon that on the face of those whom we love and who have just left us there is seen a smile of an exquisite sweetness. One does not smile when one has entered into death, but when one lives still in the moment that one is going to enter into it. This divine smile is the mark here on earth, on that which men call a dead man, or a dead woman, of a beatitude and of a life which has begun when earthly existence was about to end and which will never end.

Enumerating the reasons for which Christ has willed to die (He had come for that), St. Thomas tells us [16] that after the principal reason, which was to make atonement for us, one of the reasons was "to deliver us in dying from the fear of death."

16. *Sum. Theol.,* III, 50, 1.